What on earth should I post?

150+ Creative **Content Ideas** for your **Social Media** and **Online Marketing**

Perfect
for Entrepreneurs, Consultants and Coaches

1st edition 05/2022

Cover design: Monika Stern, sternloscreative e.U.
Cover Photo: Shutterstock
Layout and illustration: VoV media , Monika Stern, sternloscreative e.U.
Photocredit: Roman Kmenta, Shutterstock, Freepik
Editing / proofreading: VoV media
ISBN: 978-3-903845-36-7

Publisher: VoV media - www.voice-of-value.com

Prolog

This book has a long genesis. As someone who uses content marketing as a strategy and is an avid user of social media, I noticed relatively quickly that it is not that easy to always bring new, interesting, and varied content to various online channels. So, I sat down and – at first entirely for myself - made a collection of ideas for possible content.

The result was that I found a number of very useful and usable ideas for short posts and longer articles so to be able to offer something meaningful on social media and other digital channels. The next thought was that these ideas could also be of interest to my customers and online contacts, who are probably always faced with the same problem as me and ask themselves the question, "What the .... should I post?"

And so, an e-book was created with the title, "What the ... should I post?" which I distributed free of charge (to be precise, as a useful exchange item for your e-mail address for my newsletter mailing list). That must have been 2015/2016. To promote the e-book, I, of course, also distributed it on social media, often on Facebook among others.

It produced very entertaining effects. Many readers did not understand the problem and were irritated. Some were even aggressive, true to the motto, „If you don't know what to post, why don't you just shut up." Some of the comments could be described as coarse, to say the least.

Of course, I understood why. For someone who only uses Facebook privately, the option of simply not posting anything when you have nothing to say is definitely a very good and recommendable one. For people and companies who use these channels professionally as part of their content marketing strategy, not posting anything is not a real alternative.

Many commenters understood the title from a private perspective, which explains the many emotional comments. But what I still found amazing was the strong form of expression that this post triggered and the multitude of comments. Apparently, I concluded, I had hit a point there that was moving the digital network. You only write a comment if something is important. So, it was a matter of importance.

At the same time, I found it amusing that all the negative comments did the exact opposite of what they wanted to achieve. Instead of harming the post, they pushed it. They made it more interesting and increased its reach. In addition, a comment like this communicates to the Facebook algorithm that you are interested in the matter and that you would like to see more from the same author in the future.

The example also illustrates very well the interesting and unexpected dynamics that can arise in digital channels. Even a post that receives a lot of criticism can ultimately be a very good, successful post. It is not without reason that in show business they say, „It is better to be talked about badly than not at all."

And a topic that manages to move a lot of people in one way or another is worth a book. the book you hold in your hands.

AIDA - a classic with more validity than ever

Despite widespread digitalization, the classic AIDA formula for advertising effectiveness is still as valid as ever, perhaps even more so. Attention - Interest - Desire - Action. That means a customer's action, which could be a purchase, a click, a phone call, or whatever they are supposed to do, needs attention at the very beginning of this process. Attention has thus become one of the most valuable commodities in business; there is no business without attention.

Due to the rapidly advancing digitalization in all areas of life, attention is also increasingly about being perceived online, in digital form. It's about having a presence online and building a greater reach. It's about being seen by potential customers and interested parties, by the media, by future employees, by suppliers, and by the relevant public in general.

To be present online, you need content - texts, images, videos. Preferably several times a day on a wide variety of channels. The times when it was enough to post a post on Facebook once a week are long gone.

And, of course, it should be varied. It can happen that you run out of ideas for new content for blogs and posts of all kinds.

I wrote this book so that this would never happen to you again. It is a compact and extensive collection of content ideas for your online presence, for social media pages and profiles, your website, a blog, or online platforms of all kinds on which you can post.

The ideas are designed in such a way that they can be used for a wide variety of industries and subject areas. But, not everything for all areas; you choose what suits you, your products and services, your industry, and your customers. I have therefore deliberately mixed up the examples that I refer to in the book. The focus is not on the industry, but on the idea or its implementation.

In this book you will find plenty of very useful material for your online presence that you only have to adapt to your business. I can promise you that much at this point in time.

This book does a lot of the creative work for you, although you can, and should, still let your own creativity run free if you want to. I am sure you will develop entirely new content ideas based on the ideas in this book.

You can read through all the ideas and strategies in this book from start to finish and mark those that you like and that go very well with your business. The ideas section of the book (Part 2) is, however, divided into thematically coherent chapters, namely humor, things to know, employees, etc. - so that, alternatively, you can target ideas that are currently of interest to you.

The rest is planning, structure, and implementation. I will also say the most important things about this, although this is not the main subject of the book.

There is one more idea that I would like to bring closer to you at this point. The ideas in this book will seem a lot to you, especially if you have not been very active in filling your online channels with articles and posts. You might even find yourself overwhelmed by the quantity and wondering how you are going to do it alongside your actual work.

I am repeatedly confronted with this view, which is no longer current from my point of view, in my consulting and lecture practice. What we are talking about in this book is not something that needs to be added to your work, it is part of your work. With advancing digitalization, it is a part of your work that is becoming more and more important.

Gary Vaynerchuck, one of the most successful and well-known American online and social media marketing experts, repeatedly emphasizes, „All companies are media companies these days." I can 100% agree with that. If you get used to the idea of running a media company, you will find it much easier to implement the ideas and strategies in this book successfully and consistently.

I hope you enjoy reading, and hope you have lots of creative content ideas for your business.

Yours

Roman Kmenta

Before you start, get your free editorial plan

Before you start reading, visit the resources page for this book - https://www.romankmenta.com/resources-contentideas-book-english/

and get yourself further valuable information on the topic of content marketing.

There you will find:

- a list of recommendable tools that help you with your content marketing
- a free of charge editorial plan to download
- recommendations for blogs and books on the topic.

Visit the page now.

Part 1
Content Strategy and Content Planning

As announced in the prolog, I will first say a few words about topics such as content strategy and planning. This is to emphasize the significance of these things. Your ideas get lost in the digital universe if they are not based on a solid foundation, namely, your content plan.

Without a content plan, the risk is high that the posts so eagerly made at the beginning will quickly decrease and soon after ebb away and stop. That's what I keep seeing. It is therefore important to deal intensively with this topic before expanding your online presence, or even starting it.

Your content strategy and planning should answer questions such as:

- What is the goal of my online activities?
- Who do I post for? Who is my target group?
- Which channels do I want to be present on, and which not?
- In which media form(s) do I want to be present?
- What kind of content do I want to be perceived as having?
- What resources do I have for content creation and content distribution?
- How often, where, and when do I post my content; what is my editorial plan?

When you have answered these questions for yourself, you can get down to producing content and distributing it online. Not before. As with building a house, the foundation comes before the roof.

For many entrepreneurs and companies, looking at their online activities gives the impression that it is being done the other way around. First it is posted and only later, sometimes never, do they consider who it is for and why they are posting it? Accordingly, their activities seem confused and aimless and attract little to no business.

The full effects of your activities only transpire when you implement them with a goal and a plan.

Below you will find a brief summary of the most crucial things about the points mentioned above. If you have already answered all these questions for your business, you can skip some of these points.

If not, then be sure to invest the time and read this section as well. I am aware that the creative part is the more exciting one for many readers (including me) and that is why you bought the book, but, I promise you, it will definitely pay off for you to manage the above questions in advance.

If you outsource part or all of your content creation, to an agency or an employee, you have to summarize the answers to the above-mentioned questions in writing anyway so to give the agency a briefing or employee a framework within which they can move i.e., what is allowed and desired and what is not.

What is the goal of my online activities?

As with any business project worth mentioning, the question of goals should also be posed at the start of your online presence. What do you want to achieve with your posts, blogs, videos, etc.?

The following goals could be pursue:

- Increasing awareness in the relevant target group
- Establishing and strengthening an expert status
- Establishing a certain image, an image that you want to embody with the target group
- Generation of contacts (leads) for your newsletter
- Direct sales
- More traffic (visitors) to your website.

Depending on the type of business you are doing, there may, of course, be other relevant goals. The precise definition of your goal is important because the answers to many of the other questions asked earlier will depend on the goal you are pursuing.

For example, if you want to draw a lot of traffic to your website, Instagram is not a suitable channel as it does not allow a direct link from a post to your website. If your target group is people aged 65+, you can safely do without Snapchat.

Thus goals form the basis for other decisions you have to make in this context.

Who do I post for? Who is my target group?

The answer is essentially not one you should ask yourself in connection with your online presence. Rather, it is about your positioning, in which the target group definition plays an essential role.

Your target group is extremely relevant to your online presence, since you choose the media primarily depending on your target group. But the target group also has a decisive influence on the type of content and its preparation.

If you want to learn more about positioning, or to work on your positioning, you will find a lot of helpful content in „The Market Positioning Book". (https://amzn.to/2I2J9MR - as an Amazon partner, I earn from qualified sales).

When it comes to target groups and positioning, don't only think of potential customers. Suppliers, the general public and, above all, future employees should also be taken into account in your content strategy.

Regarding employees, online activities for employer branding and employee searches have become indispensable nowadays. Regardless of who you want to sell your products and services

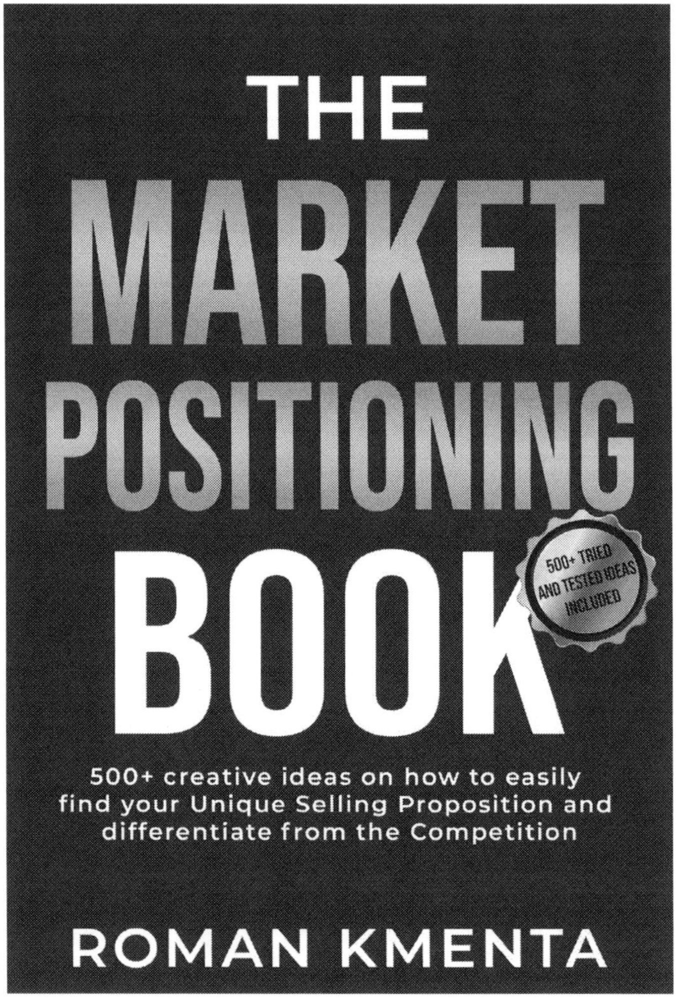

to the scope of your online activities is much greater. They have an effect on everyone who comes to you digitally online.

Which channels do I want to be present on, and which not?

As mentioned, the answer to this question is strongly related to your goals and target audience. But other factors also play a role, including:

- What form of media are you aiming for - video, audio, text, etc.? Not everything works on all channels.
- What resources do you have available? Some channels and media require less work than others, and some can even be partially automated.
- Does the image of the channel match the image of yourself you want to build or strengthen?

In general, it is advisable to choose fewer channels—initially only one—but with that one to be present fully, intensively, and professionally.

An overview of the channels

Cou can show your presence online on the below channels:

- Blogs - your own blog, and guest posts on someone else's blog
- Podcast platforms - your own, and as an interview guest in third-party podcasts
- Video platforms
    - YouTube
    - Vimeo
    - TikTok
- Social media (currently the most important)
    - Facebook
    - Instagram
    - LinkedIn
    - XING
    - Pinterest
    - Snapchat
- Online media and platforms

Each of these channels has its rules and laws. There are books and experts who specialize entirely in know-how relating to each one.

When you decide on one of the channels it is certainly a good idea to read a specialist book or get advice from an expert on establishing or expanding your presence.

In which media form do I want to be present?

Regardless of different content, you can bring a lot of variety to your media presence just through the presentation and preparation of your content.

In principle, you can use all display variants, but not all are suitable for all content. However, you can implement some content several times in different ways. You should do this to make the most of your time and other resources.

You can use the following basic forms of representation for your content:

Text

This can be normally written text or - as a special - also text that was created in a graphics program / editor (e.g. integrated in Facebook) and saved or displayed as an image.

Image

There are various possibilities and variants of display forms for images:

- **Photos** (own or third-party / purchased) - often also edited, for example:
    - Color changed through the use of filters (as you can find them in your smartphone camera and in all graphics and presentation programs)
    - With added text
    - Changed by graphics
- **Drawings** -
  generated by hand or computer
  Hand drawings and sketches in particular can be very suitable in terms of attention. In an increasingly "optically perfect" media world (making clean graphics has become much easier thanks to the support of graphics programs), something as original as a hand-drawn sketch is easier to get noticed.
- **Infographics**
  Infographics aren't just more complex images. They are, when done well, a lot more. You can represent or add to longer texts in a simple form. They are very common on channels like Pinterest but can also be used in others. Creating a good infographic is relatively complex. However, the investment of time can be worth your while.

But you don‘t necessarily have to do it yourself, or have it done. There are already databases with pre-produced infographics (https://infog-rapia.com/) that at least partially do the work for you.

Video / film

There are two versions of the video that can be distinguished:

- Pre-recorded and uploaded to the channel
- As a live stream, common on some social media (Facebook, Instagram, YouTube etc.)

The combination of the two variants is not only possible, but also makes sense regarding the efficient use of resources - first create a live stream, then save this live video and upload it to other channels.

GIF (Graphics Interchange Format)

A GIF is a special form of image; a kind of an-imation lasting a few seconds.

Audio

Audio files—live or studio recordings-—are mostly used on podcast platforms (such as iTunes). The combination with video is often used here. For example, an interview can be recorded as a live video. The soundtrack is then saved separately and used as a podcast episode.

Slideshow

Slideshows occupy a special position in the media presentation world and therefore deserve a separate mention. They are automated presentations that can be stored with speech or music. The most famous platform for slideshows is www.slideshare.com from LinkedIn.

Saved in the appropriate format, slideshows can also be used on other channels.

E-book

A very special, digital form of representation that is becoming more and more popular is the e-book. Publishing an e-book—once the content has been written—is not particularly difficult or time-consuming. There are a number of platforms and ways to get your e-books to your target audience. One is as a simple PDF download on your website, for example, which you promote via your social media channels and your newsletter. E-books are often offered in exchange for the contact‘s e-mail address.

You can also offer and sell the e-book as a purchase product via Amazon or other e-book shops.

This not only increases your reach, but also earns you money. A professionally written e-book with interesting and helpful content does a lot more than a blog or a short post for your expert status.

Which of them suits you?

The media forms of presentation that you should use in your online presence are also related to several of the other questions that basically need to be answered.

It's about the answers to the question, how well does a form of representation fit your:

- **Content**
- **Products or services**
  A speaker should definitely use the medium of video in some way, photos are a must for a photographer.
- **Image**
  Some forms of media appear more conservative, modern, dynamic, calmer, etc. than others. The presentation of your content naturally rubs off on your image.
- **Know-how in terms of production**
  A graphic designer finds it much easier to create infographics than someone without graphics knowledge.
- **Resources**
  If you already have a video studio, videos are easy to make.
- **Customers**
- **Preferences**
  One could also ask which form of presentation do you like more?
  Do you like to write, or are you a fanatical video filmmaker with your smartphone? Everything you love to do will be easiest for you.

Here, too, it should be noted how closely all these questions are interlinked.

What kind of content do I want to be noticed with?

One question that you should clarify in advance is what kind of content you want to be perceived online with. That content also has to match the points listed above. Ultimately, your online presence must result in a coherent overall picture in itself and with your target group.

There are a few fundamental decisions that need to be made.

Personal or just business?

Do you want to show yourself online personally or privately, as a person and - to a certain extent to be defined - also allow insights into your private life? If so, how far do you want to go? And if you want to do that, does it only affect you, or does it also affect your partner or family?

Or will you say strictly "no" to personal and private insights, limit yourself to your business or company in your postings and completely exclude personal information?There are valid arguments for both.

What speaks for personal insights is that potential customers, or the relevant public, can more easily establish an emotional connection with people than with companies. You also have many more creative options and topics for your content if you don't exclude personal information.

However, I can understand anyone who thinks that their private life is nobody's business and plans to focus entirely on business content. This question is one that self-employed people and small business owners in particular need to be clear about. In corporations, personal insights into the private lives of senior management are not expected (although that could be an exciting and eye-catching strategy).

In this context, you should also consider the following questions:

- How much humor, and of what kind, do you want to use?
- Is politics allowed in your content?
- Do you want to refer to current events and situations; topics that move the world a lot?

Once you have clarified your position on these, it will be much easier for you to create content efficiently and consistently for your posts and contributions.

What resources do I have for content creation and distribution?

Content production is a matter of the resources that are available to you. The question of resources has has already been raised at one point or another, so let's examine few more detailed words on this.

You can, indeed must, use the following types of resources to create content for your online presence:

- Time - your own, that of your employees, or that of a service provider / agency, or all three
- Money
- Things and premises - this can be an already existing video or sound studio
- Know-how - such knowledge or skills that you can already access in yourself or in your employees, including the creation of videos and photos, graphic skills, or writing skills.

Things are not usually a bottleneck because you can buy most of what you need relatively cheaply. A small video setting is feasible in sufficient quality with an investment of $1,000 - 2,000 Of course, there are no upper limits. The technical equipment for a podcast won't cost you more than $200 if you already own a laptop.

The question of time is the most delicate. If your own time is limited, then you should choose forms of representation that do not necessarily require your direct input.

Anyone on your team can write a text, but you should probably conduct an interview yourself.

If you're short on time and cash, outsourcing many (but not all) of the things related to content creation can help.

Content-Recycling

An extremely important point that I would like to address briefly and separately is the topic of content recycling, the efficient, multiple use of the same content. Cleverly and with a plan, you can reduce your workload by 50, 60, or even 70% through content recycling.

Let me demonstrate this procedure using an example.

1. You come up with a series of questions that your customers ask, or might ask, more often than others along with your answers to them. If you can't think of anything, ask your customers what topics or questions they are interested in. If you answer these questions e.g. address them to your community on Facebook, these posts and the comments on them are interesting content in themselves.
2. You then answer these questions e.g. in a Facebook live video that you announce in advance, and this is something you can post again. You can add a title and e.g. a serial number, because it is part of a series, and post it on Facebook.
3. Then download the video and upload it to YouTube and LinkedIn (or other channels where video is possible). Thus, you can fill your YouTube channel with minimal additional effort.
4. You can also cut out short sequences from the video and use these „video snippets" as your post on suitable platforms, and thus turn a video into a number of posts.
5. You can have the video transcribed for little money, or you can use suitable software to do it if you speak clearly enough and the sound quality is good enough. You can then add a suitable picture to this transcription as a blog post on your website, or, even better, embed the video on your blog and put it online.
6. From there you can also distribute it to your other channels, such as XING, Twitter etc. (where it is technically easily possible).

7. If you optimize the blog post according to SEO (Search Engine Optimization) criteria, you will be found more easily on Google and will get visitors to your website.

8. You can filter out the soundtrack from the video (tools like Zoom, which you can also use for the Facebook live video, do this automatically) and use it as a podcast episode.

9. As soon as you have a number of these episodes, you can turn them into an audiobook, which you can promote as a freebie (free product) in exchange for the email address on your website (and of course on all your channels) andalso offer them as a digital purchase product on suitable platforms and earn a little money with it directly.

10. You can also have the audio book pressed onto CD, which is quite inexpensive (<$1 per item). You then have a physical product that you can sell at events for around $10-20. At the same time, such a CD is also very suitable as a small gift for customers or interested parties.

11. Since people not only hear but also read, you can publish the collection of transcriptions as an e-book. Like the audio book, you can use this in digital form as a freebie to expand your address list. You can also use the e-book for Kindle or in other formats on suitable platforms such as Amazon, for example offer for sale at $1-10and earn money with it again.

12. You can also have the e-book printed as a booklet or even a book at low cost (from around $2), depending on how much material you have collected, to sell at events for $10-20 or give away to customers.

13. With the book you can go to classic media outlets and try to make them report about you. These articles and reports in turn are something that you can scan in and distribute on your digital channels.

14. At the same time, you can put small topics or chapters of the book in the form of a column in a newspaper or magazine, or make a longer article out of several topics, according to the motto “The best answers to the ten most burning questions about XY.” When this is published, you will again have material to post.

As you can see, the list is almost endless and self-reinforcing. All your activities result in something that you can use again for a new post or contribution. Be a little creative and, most importantly, make your life as easy as possible when it comes to creating and using your content. The greatest effort is incurred when creating new content. So, use what you have instead of always reinventing everything.

Small bites rather than large chunks

Rapidly advancing digitalization has not only made the world faster, it has also generated other effects. The constantly increasing speed means that we have less and less time to read or process large chunks of content. A short post with –one to two sentences, one photo, and one entertaining 30 second video is quickly read or viewed. Our communication online has become much shorter in recent years.

This means rethinking for everyone who wants to increase their reach online. On many channels, but not all, the motto is "more and shorter content."

But that also has advantages for you. For example, from a 60-minute interview - which you can find on some channels such as YouTube, can and should show in its full length, then you can cut out 10 or 20 short sequences and make many small posts from them.

In the book I refer to these as content bites over and over again. A bite is something that your audience can consume in passing and easily digest.

Content distribution

It's also important to consider content distribution when planning your resources. You can produce the best content, but if no one or too few contacts are seeing them, the return will ultimately be low.

It is said, as a rule of thumb, that the same amount of time has to be planned for the professional digital distribution of the content as for the creation. For example, if you spend one day on the creation of a large blog article, you should plan another day, not necessarily in one go, to share this article on all your channels, and those of others. The work involved in distributing digital content is very often underestimated.

To prevent that from happening, be sure to read the following section.

How often and when do I post my content where? - The editorial plan

The creation of content is only part of the work needed for your online presence. The second part, which takes about as much time and effort, is the distribution of the content. You should definitely summarize both in an editorial plan. Without an editorial schedule, the chances are that your online activities will fizzle out very quickly.

An editorial plan is an indispensable planning and control tool for you, especially when your employees take on part of the creation and the complete distribution of your content.

Editorial plan structure

Such a plan is not technically demanding. In the simplest case it regulates:

- what
- when
- where
- and by whom it is posted.

You can create it Excel, for example, by entering the days of the week in the columns and the time in the rows, as in a calendar. Then enter the individual activities in the cells.

There can, and will be, recurring activities. For example, posting a teaser from the weekly blog post on Facebook on Thursday at 10 a.m. There will also be one-off activities related to special occasions, for example, Mother's Day, school starting, the publication of a new book, the promotion of a seminar, etc..

Recurring activities make your job alot easier. You could also post on a different topic every day. For a fitness trainer this could be:

- Monday: Motivation
- Tuesday: Legs
- Wednesday: Nutrition
- Thursday: Upper body
- Friday: Training with others
- Saturday: Arms
- Sunday: Relaxation

So, Monday could look like this on Facebook:

- 08:00 - LIVE morning exercises
- 10:00 - Post a motivational quote as a picture
- 12:00 - Motivation tip for „eating healthier"
- 15:00 - Before and after picture of clients who have become fitter
- 18:00 - Question to fans: What did you do for your fitness today?

An editorial plan could look like this, or something similar. The same details must then be planned for the other channels and the other days. You can already see that there is definitely work involved here. What makes the implementation even more demanding is that certain activities have to be carried out at certain times of the day.

So, it doesn't make a lot of sense if you work through everything that we have planned in the above example during the day between 8 a.m. and 10 a.m. There is also a right time to make posts on social media, and sensibly distributed is definitely better than posting everything at once.

You can also find a sample of the editorial plan for download in the resources area of this book.

https://www.romankmenta.com/resources-contentideas-book-english/

You can make this work easier for yourself by using the below strategies.

Prepare your content in time blocks

If we look at our sample for Monday above, we can see that most of the posts can be prepared in advance. All except the live morning exercises, if you really want to be live. Prepare the posts in blocks. What do I mean by that?

Don't work out a motivational quote at 9:30 a.m. on Monday and post it at 10 a.m. The effort is too big. Instead, prepare 100 or even 200 quotes ready to go so, you have material prepared for many Mondays, or many months if you also post quotes on other days of the week. This way, the workload per post is much lighter.

By the way, content recycling in its simplest form can also be used for this. When you are done with the quotes after 6 or 12 months, just start over with the same ones. Nobody will notice, especially since the crowd of your contacts and fans is constantly changing. Whatever you do will only ever be noticed by a relatively small part of the potential target group. If, for example, you have 1,000 Facebook fans, the quote will probably not even be seen by 20 people. And even if someone notices it, it doesn't do any harm. You can read a good quote over and over again.

However, you should not only carefully plan the creation, but also the preparation for the distribution of the posts. It is best to pre-program your editorial plan for the whole week. You can find out how to do this below.

Outsource work to employees or service providers

Outsource all activities related to your posts that are easy and inexpensive to outsource. This can affect the creation of the content on the one hand, but also the distribution on the other.

To stick with our quotation example, unless you happen to be a graphic artist you shouldn't do the 200 quotations yourself, and if you are a graphic artist, you still shouldn't. Your time is too valuable for that.

Create one or more templates for quotations with a suitable look and commission someone to enter the 200 quotations and save them as an image. You can also outsource the search for quotations. You can make the selection yourself. It's quick and easy.

Automate parts of this work

In this context, automation means outsourcing the distribution of your content to suitable software tools on the various platforms that you use. This is primarily about social media channels, as this is where the bulk of your posts take place. Many, but not all, social media platforms allow the use of software.

Some prohibit it under threat of consequences, which can range from temporarily blocking your account to expelling you. So, be careful about which tools you use, where, and for what. Tools that simply post the content you have created on the planned days at the right time, Hootsuite for example, are harmless in my view.

With a tool like Hootsuite, you can pre-program all of your posts for different social media platforms for the whole week, or for several weeks. Not only is this very convenient, but it's essential if you post a lot.

A list of different tools can be found in the resources section of this book.

https://www.romankmenta.com/resources-contentideas-book-english/

How much is too much?

A question that is often asked and that affects your editorial plan is, "How much is too much? How many posts should there be, and how many are too many?" There is no clear answer. On the one hand, it depends very much on the medium. So, you can post 10 or 20 tweets per day on Twitter without attracting too much attention and certainly not in a negative way. Twitter is a very fast-moving medium. On Facebook, you're probably doing well with three to five posts a day right now.

What is even more important in this context is what you post. There isn't one too many, but there is one that's too uninteresting. There can hardly be too many of really exciting, entertaining, and varied posts. And that is exactly what this book is about—creating varied content that your contacts like to read, see, or hear.

After we have dealt with these questions, which are crucial for your online success, we can now turn to the core topic of the book, namely, "What can you post, and what possibilities and ideas are there for interesting content?"

Part 2
Content-Creation and Content-Ideas

Tips for content creation

Before we turn to the specific suggestions for your posts and contributions, I will give you a few tips and instructions on how to deal with the many ideas that you will find listed below.

The reason why content gets high reach

To get the best possible reach and attention from your ideas, it helps a lot to put yourself in the shoes of the potential readers and ask yourself two questions:

- Why do people share or like certain content?
- What kind of content is shared or liked and how much (which of course is closely related to the first question)?

The answers to these questions have to do with three things in particular:

- The motivation of the people who see or read posts and contributions
- The design and preparation of the contributions (graphics, wording, etc.)
- The media implementation or form of presentation as text, photo, graphics, video etc.

According to a study based on almost 1,500 answers, the three most common answers, and thus the main reasons why we promote certain content, are:

1. Because I find it interesting / entertaining (45% women / 44% men)
2. Because I think it's helpful to others (33% women / 26% men - which suggests that women may have a stronger motive to help)
3. Because it made me laugh (13% women / 17% men)

Even if these numbers look a little different in other studies, they still give us a basic idea of the motives of your contacts when it comes to dealing with content.

There are also tons of studies, blog posts, and books on the subject of „How do you design posts and contributions so that they are clicked and shared?" This is also an exciting and important topic but it is not covered in this book. I can, however, recommend anyone who wants to get more coverage to deal with it. In the resources area you will find some additional articles linked.

https://www.romankmenta.com/resources-contentideas-book-english/

As mentioned, the third success factor is the chosen form of presentation. The same piece of content may not be of interest to anyone as text, but as a video it may become a star in your network. There are always changing trends in forms of presentation. Video is very popular right now, but that doesn't mean pure text posts can't perform very well. Above all, the form of presentation must match the content.

Instructions for working with ideas

In this second part of the book you will find a huge number of ideas for your posts. You will probably only be able to use part of it for your venture, since by far not all ideas will meet the conditions that you defined for your business in the first part of the book. Still, I can promise you, there will be more than enough for you to use.

The ideas are divided into subject areas. These sometimes overlap, which is unavoidable but also planned and useful. Completely new content can arise from the combination of several ideas.

Let your creativity run wild and deal with those ideas that at first glance seem unsuitable or strange. Sometimes, it is precisely those that can represent a real treasure trove for your business.

Above all, remember to check every idea for a post or series in terms of its feasibility in various media forms of presentation. This is how a small idea quickly turns into many posts.

For support, you will find the forms of representation briefly summarized as a checklist below:

- Text
- Image
  - Photo (own or third-party / purchased)
  - Drawings - generated by hand or computer
  - Infographics
- Video / Film
  - pre-recorded
  - as a live stream
- GIF (Graphics Interchange Format)
- Audio
- Slide show

Produce a series of posts

Many ideas also have the potential to be turned into a series, that is, to create a few or many posts from them, which you can then publish over a longer period of time, often at regular intervals.

A variant of the series concept is to make "more of the same." For example, review a book every week and post this review, and the recommendations become a series of a particular kind.

But you can also split a longer activity into successive parts and turn them into a series of posts. For example,f you are a builder, you can document the construction of a house—from the idea to the planning to the finished house—and publish it as a series of posts.

Google alerts

An indispensable tool for you is Google Alerts. There, you can enter all the terms that might interest you in connection with your company, including:

- Your name
- Competitors' names
- Customers' and suppliers' names
- Own products (with name or product description) or competitors' products
- Terms are related to what you do (in the case of a window manufacturer, these could include building a house, renovation, thermal insulation, etc.).

Google will then send you a message by e-mail, and you can specify how often you want to receive an e-mail, every time one of these terms appears on the internet (). This is not only very practical for sales, market, and competitor monitoring, but also for getting material and ideas for articles and postings.

And, don't worry, you can always delete, add, and change the terms if you find that you're getting too much material that you can't use.

Creativity sprawling

With all of the many creative ideas in this book, plus those that will come to you as you read it, you should always keep an eye on the goals of your posts and contributions. It's not about making a lot of posts and being active at all costs. Rather, it's about making many good posts, and a post is good if it helps achieve the content marketing goals you have set.

I would like to repeat this in particular, because when I was writing the book I noticed that creativity can be sprawling, and that you can sometimes lose sight of your actual goals when enthusiastically creating content for digital channels.

From simple to complex

In line with this note, which concerns excessive creativity, some ideas can be implemented very easily, and others take a lot of effort (in money or time) to implement.

Simple ideas are often those where you take something that already exists and turn it into content for your channels - e.g. a selfie of you at work. More elaborate ideas are often based on something that you first have to bring into being - e.g. your own award that you give regularly. Both are possible and also useful, especially since you can usually get much more content out of the ideas that are associated with more effort in the form of entire series and a wide variety of content.

To make it easy to recognize, all ideas below are marked with one to three points, which denote both the time (⏱) and the financial ($) effort.

⏱ = can be implemented without any significant time expenditure

⏱⏱ = can be implemented with a little time expenditure

⏱⏱⏱ = can be implemented with considerable time expenditure

$ = can be implemented at no cost

$$ = can be implemented with a little financial effort
$$$ = can be implemented at considerable cost

These values are estimates realistically based on a minimal to average effort. Of course, it depends very much on the execution and implementation of the tip. For example, you can have an expert interview with little effort, e.g. lead via Zoom or Skype and record or invite the experts to a studio and have a professional video created there with two cameras and extensive post-processing.

The examples

Some of the specific examples given are those that have achieved a large reach, while some are just moderately successful. Above all, I wanted to use these examples to show how the ideas I am currently writing about were implemented. Furthermore, I didn't want to give the impression that every post has to be extremely well received. This is also not the case with the very successful online players. That would frustrate you unnecessarily.

Rather, you should generate a background noise with an average of successful posts and every now and then you will get a hit in the form of a post with far above average success. And if you have a solid strategy and implement it consistently, and are creative and try out different ideas, the above-average successes will increase over time.

What can be described as successful, especially in connection with online channels, depends very much on the size of the existing network and the number of contacts and fans or, in the case of blog posts, the strength of the website. For someone with 1,000 fans on Facebook, 50 likes for a post may be very respectable. For someone with 10,000 fans it is normal, and for a page with 100,000 fans, it's a poor performance.

Numbering

For easier retrieval, all ideas and strategies are consecutively numbered across chapters. So, you only need to write down a number and you will find the idea again very quickly at any time.

Warning notice on data protection and rights

Some of the ideas, especially those that show people or name names, could be sensitive from a privacy perspective. If in doubt, clarify with a data protection expert whether, and in what form, an idea can be implemented for you. For some it will be necessary to obtain the explicit, often written, consent of a person.

As far as any rights to the materials used are concerned, you must also clarify this on a case-by-case basis if it concerns texts, images, or videos from others. Using third-party content, especially third-party images, without obtaining consent or purchasing the material can be very expensive.

A.

Personal

This area is about personal items, maybe even very personal. Whether, and how far, you want to use this pool of ideas for your business is a fundamental decision for you. Some do just that, very intensively, others don‘t say a word about private or personal matters.

Basically, the following ideas are always about talking about yourself in some form, revealing something, perhaps also secret, confidential.

1. Personal goals

🕐**$**

What do you want to achieve and by when? Why do you want to achieve something? You can bring up the topic of your own goal achievement over and over again and report regularly on how you are progressing towards a goal.

2. Your beginnings and your history

🕐**$**

This could be a kind of short biography, presented in words and pictures, seasoned with old photos which could be presented very well as a series. This idea is particularly interesting if you rely on yourself as a personal brand and practice personal branding. The better known you are already the more people will be interested in learning more about you.

3. Hobbies

🕐**$**

Hobbies are a real fund of ideas for posts. Much can also be represented in sound, images and text. Hobbies connect people who have the same interests very strongly. People report on classy old-timers, their hobby cooking skills, the quality of different cigars, the marathons they run and also their collections of old postcards and receive a lot of attention and likes in the various networks.

4. Vacation and travel

🕐🕐**$$**

If you want to report on a trip on your channels, it is advisable to create a concept for it beforehand. I know from my own experience that you can quickly become overwhelmed. You are in a vacation mood and not in a work mood, there are plenty of impressions, and you ask yourself, “What should I report on now?”

For example, a style consultant taking a trip to New York could create a series on the topic „Fashion shopping in Manhattan - the most unusual stores.“ With this concept in mind, you go through the city in a completely different way and look for and find many great examples that fit into this concept.

Of course, you could also have two or more parallel concepts for posts about your vacation. At some point, however, the question rightly arises, "Is this still a vacation, or, is it a business trip that you took for just that purpose.?

5. Family, partner, and children

⏱$

If it's what you want and you've made the decision to do it, your family, especially your children, have plenty of scope for content. This is particularly interesting if your products and services have anything to do with children (children's clothing, toys etc.).

6. Vice

⏱$

Most people have vices. I'm not talking about the big ones like a gambling addiction that ruins your existence, but the little ones, the everyday ones. An excess of sweets, a weakness for wine, beer, whiskey (without being an alcoholic), cigars etc. You can also see your vices as something that makes you stand out as a person. You can drink your beer in silence or document the drinking and enjoyment of different types of beer online.

7. Daily routines / your daily routine

⏱$

Daily routines, from getting up to going to bed, are something everyone has. Exciting content for your fans can be created from it if you report on it in a targeted manner. Every hour or minute, with live videos and photos. Maybe your fans have always wanted to know how you brush your teeth, by hand or electrically?

8. Relaxation

⏱$

In line with the previous point, relaxation routines are also something you can develop content from. Of course, you have to make sure that these are still relaxing for you.

9. Values and principles

⏱$

What drives you in life? In your job? What is important to you? Your values t can also be turned into very personal content. And it doesn't stop at values. The value "reliability," for example, means something different for everyone. What does reliability mean for you translated into very concrete, practical examples?

10. Social projects and activities

⏱$

Do you support any social projects and activities? Maybe even some that you started? Report on them. This has the added benefit that you can do something for these projects at the same time.

11. Role models

⏱$

What role models do you have in different areas of life? What makes these people role models for you? That would also have the potential for a small series of contributions.

12. Clothing

⏱$

Let the digital world take a look into your closet. What do you wear often? Why? What have you bought and never worn? With the latter you could even make a competition and e.g. for example, raffle an item of clothing online every week, and put it in social media content, that you have never worn. Perhaps you can even get others excited about the idea and turn it into a community action.

13. Preferences

⏱$

What do you like, and what do you dislike? In many ways, your preferences are a repository for posts and content of all kinds. These can be preferences from all possible areas, including:

- Blogs, YouTube channels, or podcasts; campaigns can, of course, be carried out together with the respective operators or authors
- TV and movie stars
- Series and films
- Authors and books
- Post about a book you are currently reading
- Food and drink
- Particularly with food and drink you can do the opposite, post what you don‘t like, for example your top 10 most disgusting foods or drink.
- Music and musicians
- Painters and artists
- Vacation spots.

14. You at work

🕐$

Depending on the type of your business, you can use photos or a short video of yourself doing your work well as content for short posts. That would be a special part of your daily routine, so to speak, which we have already mentioned above.

15. The most pleasant / uncomfortable task

🕐$

There are also more or less pleasant activities in the things you do. So, for example, you could report on the most unpleasant task every day.

16. Selfies

🕐$

Selfies have probably become the most popular photos taken and posted in recent years. You could almost call it an art form in its own right. A selfie itself has no real content and makes no statement.

Selfies are quite interesting as a form of representation in connection with one of the ideas already mentioned or those below.
Selfies while traveling, such as you in front of the top ten sights in a city, for example. Selfies are a very useful tool, especially with a pronounced personal branding strategy.

B.

Your company

If your business is not just about you and your home office, it is an especially rich source of all kinds of content. As you will see in this chapter, you can find out about and report on a great deal of interesting and entertaining information.

17. Company presentation

🕐🕐**$**

The classic company presentation is neither unusual nor new, but you can still turn it into valuable content, for example in the form of a video or a slide presentation.

18. Company news

🕐**$**

Company news has a bad reputation for being the only thing many companies bring to their websites in the way of news. It is definitely too little and mostly too unspectacular. In addition, little reference is made to the needs and benefits of customers.

For social media channels, on the other hand, news from your company is perfectly suitable for turning into content for fresh posts, especially if you manage to give the post a human touch. That means instead of just posting, "We won the XY award," also showing the employees who have earned the award beaming with joy at the award ceremony.

19. A look behind the scenes

🕐**$**

A look behind the scenes of your company can be anything. In a production company, for example, it would be exciting to show how and in which work steps the products are manufactured. For a service provider you can show the implementation of the service in the form of small content snippets. Both have the potential to be turned into a series of articles.

20. Company values

🕐🕐**$**

Does your company have a vision, a mission, or documented corporate values according to which you operate your business? Turn it into content for your digital channels. It is not enough to post the formulated vision / mission statement or your company values on Facebook. This is boring.

It would be much more interesting to use specific examples to show how you live your vision and your values on a daily basis. To say you work sustainably is one thing; to post how a joint effort by the employees has succeeded in significantly reducing the plastic waste in the offices and documenting this with before and after photos is completely different.

21. Company goals

⏱$

The goals that you pursue with your company are suitable for creating online content in two ways. First, there are the goals themselves that you could communicate to the digital public. Second, you can report regularly on how you are doing in the implementation of your goals.

This is something that listed stock corporations have to do, and do in detail, in the form of monthly, quarterly, and annual reports, albeit but mostly in a form very precisely defined by stock corporation law.

Companies and entrepreneurs who do not have to do it, could do. Some self-employed and small business owners publish their monthly sales on their website—Pat Flynn, an American media entrepreneur and podcaster, did this for a while.

22. Milestones

⏱$

In line with the topic of goals, it makes sense to communicate or celebrate partial goals and milestones online. When the book that you wanted to write is finally ready, or the website is online in its new form, for example.

Stefan James of Project Life Mastery not only communicated his annual goals via video on his YouTube channel, but he also made a detailed, monthly report on the status of his goal achievement: https://www.youtube.com/watch?v=Zm4UEJczu9s

23. Commitment to a good cause

⏱$

Supporting social, ecological, or charitable projects can also result in interesting content for company posts.

24. Your other social media profiles

⏱$

The networking of the various digital channels that you use and play on is also something that you can specifically force and make your own contributions from. For example, you can make a Facebook post under the title “Best of Instagram” in which you show your Facebook friends and fans the best photos that you have put online on Instagram, coupled with the request that they, too, visit Instagram. This is especially useful if you don‘t share exactly the same content on all of your channels.

25. Company history

🕐🕐$

Above all, companies with a long tradition and decades of history have a lot to tell in retrospect. You can turn it into a slideshow, movie, or even a book. But you can also turn it into a lot more material for posts by breaking the story down into small pieces. Every single photo from your company history, every single newspaper article, and every single event can be a separate article for your online channels. Here too, a series could be made out of it, for example, “Looking back - impressions from the last 50 years.”

26. Promotional gifts and giveaways

🕐$

Good, humoros content can even be created from something quite banal in itself, such as promotional gifts. For example, if you offer towels as freebies, you could take a picture of the company outing to the beach with all the participants wrapped in the company towels. Or you can hire a group of young people, as the construction company i + R has done very nicely.

If you have many different giveaways, you can even make a small series of them and show them in a variety of ways. What can you use your great towel for more or less sensibly?

https://www.instagram.com/p/Bype7HPC6pG/

C.

Company goals

One category of content that people online are particularly interested in is other people. What they do, where, with whom, what they say, and what they think. We humans are communal animals. It is therefore a good idea to include your employees in your content, not only when creating the content, but also you can let your employees become the content themselves, always provided that they want to.

27. Introduce employees

🕐$

The easiest way to involve your employees in your content is to introduce them. You can do this individually or in small groups, for example, by department. You can apply many of the ideas for posts that we discussed about yourself in the "Personal" chapter above to your employees. Let them create these posts themselves. Some people will be enthusiastic about such a project. You can use all the common media possibilities including text, video, and photos.

28. Job vacancies / recruitment

🕐$

Digital channels have become an integral part of the search for employees. These not only help you find new employees, but—when cleverly done—you can also create interesting content with them.

Instead of just posting a job advertisement, you can:

- let employees speak who are already doing this job
- photograph the workplace
- photograph or film an employee in their daily work in the job to be filled and document the most important tasks in some areas
- introduce future colleagues.

With a little creativity and humor, you can achieve an effect that is far greater than what a simple job description or job advertisement can offer.

29. New employees

🕐$

If a new employee comes on board, that is a great opportunity to produce digital content. For example, the new employee could document their first X days in the form of a digital diary and make daily posts from it. The format for this should be specified, then it will also be easier for the employee. Contents could be:

- What did you learn today?

- What were you amazed about today?
- What were you most happy about today? Etc.

30. Employees who leave

⏱$

Even in the best companies it regularly happens that employees leave the company. Sometimes because they are retiring, sometimes because they are moving to another company or starting their own business. How these are handled show companies in a very special light. If you manage to organize this separation in such a way that neither the employee nor the company harbor negative feelings, you can also use this event for postings. For example, you could include the departing employee in your search for a successor and include them in the above-mentioned ideas on the subject of recruiting.

31. Employee anniversaries

⏱$

An employee doesn't have to be new or even leave to be celebrated. All kinds of anniversaries are also suitable for this. These can be the classic membership anniversaries - 10, 20, 25 years, etc.,but why wait so long? Who says that you can't also post the one-week, one-month or one-year anniversary in the digital world?

32. Birthdays

⏱$

Your employees' birthdays fall into the same category. Why not come up with a nice ritual such as cake with candles and birthday serenades, in the simplest case, document this on photo or video (or even implement it as a live video) and post it in suitable channels? This could result in sympathetic and often funny (depending on the ritual) contributions.

33. Weddings

⏱$

For many people, weddings are something too private and beyond what one would like to stage in the media. However, some, especially celebrities and VIPs, do it anyway and get a lot of content and attention. Whether it is still within the green range for you and, in this case, your employees to turn the wedding into a media event must be decided on a case-by-case basis.

Of course, some general conditions where it is very tempting to use employee weddings, or your own, for your content marketing. Anywhere the company has something to do with weddings, it's definitely worth considering.

That could be the case with:

- bridal shops
- wedding photographers
- rental of typical wedding locations
- event caterers with an emphasis on hosting weddings
- jewelers
- etc.The German social media expert Felix Beilharz shows how the sensitive topic of weddings can be implemented very simply but effectively with a lot of tact with a post that just contains “She said yes” as a message. He received hundreds of likes and comments and sympathy points for this.

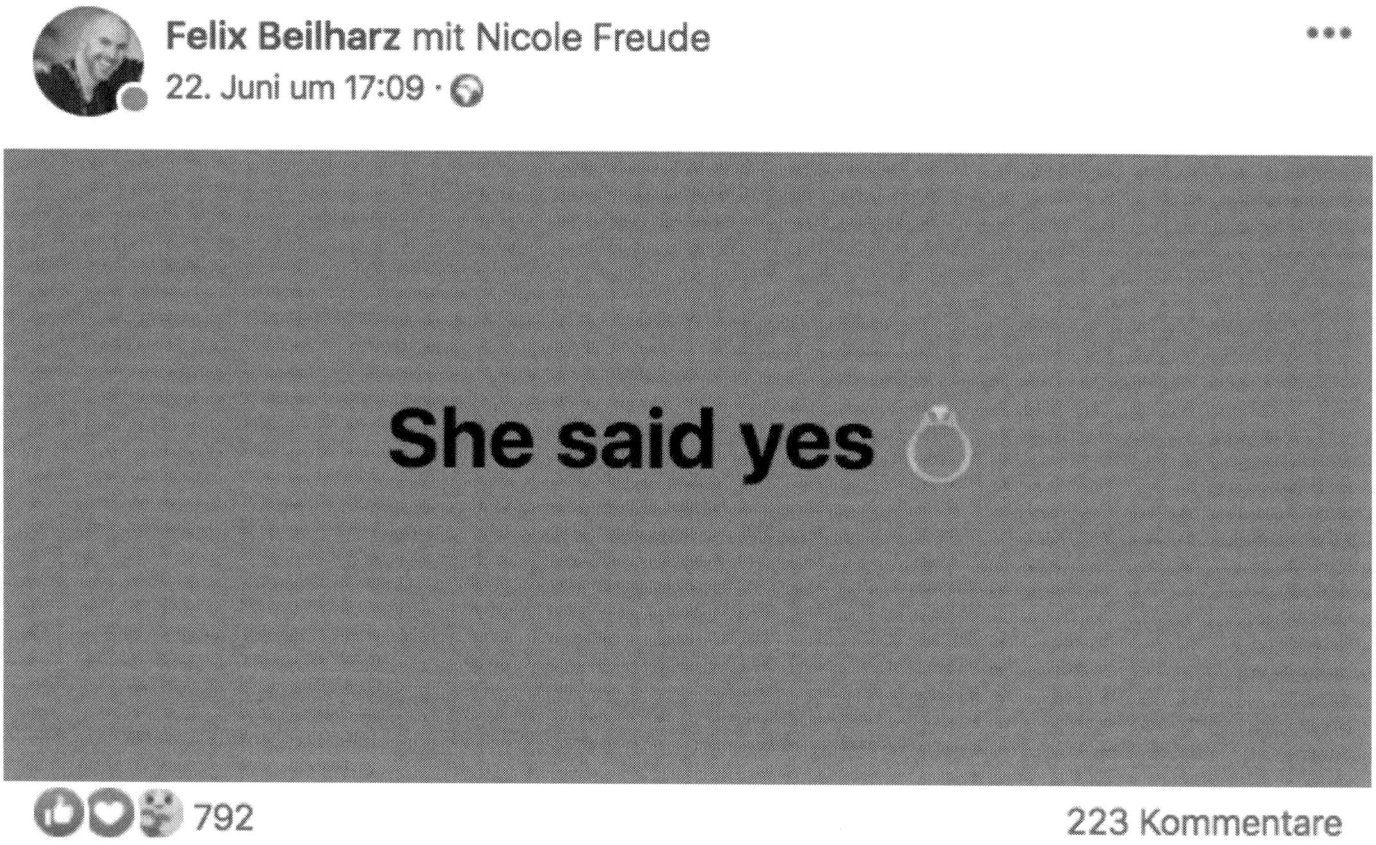

https://www.facebook.com/felix.beilharz/posts/4693407154018774

34. Employee of the month

⏱⏱$

Many companies choose an employee of the month. This is selected based on various performance-related criteria. Usually a photo of the employee is shown in the entrance area or the canteen. Why not communicate this award on social media as well?

But there is more to the concept. If you differentiate, for example, the type of service for which an award is made, you can have not just one but several employees per month.

A few examples of this are:

- the one with the best new idea
- the one with the best customer feedback
- the one with the greatest commitment
- the one who made the mistake from which the company learned the most (for companies with the appropriate error culture).

Of course, there could be more humorous categories if that fits the image that you want to radiate.

For larger companies, you could also break down the 'Employee of the Month' categories by department or division. Even an "employee of the day" could be conceivable if he can be easily identified. This would give you a message every day that is worth at least one post, provided your team is big enough that people don't repeat themselves over and over again.

In the case of very large companies with a correspondingly large number of executives, there could also be an executive of the month whose performance is reported online.

35. Swap profiles

⏱⏱$

One of the special features of Instagram is that you can only create posts on your smartphone; it is not possible from a desktop or laptop computer (although I know there are workarounds). Therefore, Instagram profiles are always assigned to a mobile device. So, if you have a company smartphone on which your company Instagram profile runs, then this will be looked after by one person.

Why not give this smartphone to different employees on a daily or weekly basis, who are then responsible for the company's Instagram profile during this time? Of course, this requires a concept and a framework so that employees know what to do and what doesn't fit. This could create a lot of varied content.

The same procedure is also conceivable for other social media channels and is also used there.

36. Company animals and mascots

⏱$

Some companies have company animals or mascots, often stuffed animals. These, the living ones, as well as those made of fabric, can be used wonderfully for company postings. Content that shows animals is received as particularly sympathetic and likes to be liked and shared.

The event agency 'Happy & Ness' from Vienna often puts the agency dog Stella in the limelight in photos, videos, in action, in disguise, and suitable for all occasions. There's nowhere that Stella doesn't fit.

If you do not have a company animal or do not want to get one especially for the purpose of content production, which would not be the right motivation to become a pet owner, then you can use a suitable fabric mascot, e.g. a teddy bear, a dog, etc. and put it in the limelight in your posts.

https://bit.ly/3a0ckdf

37. Employee events

⏱$

As part of all kinds of company events, your employees can also be used again for entertaining, humorous, and informative content and postings. The Christmas party (if not too much alcohol has flowed), the company outing, Mardi Gras / Carnival or Halloween offer a variety of ideas for content.

38. Training events

⏱⏱$

All types of seminars, workshops, and events that serve to further educate employees not only offer plenty of opportunities for interesting content, but also communicate that work is being done on the quality of the company's employees. And that in turn is not only in the interests of the company, but also in the interests of the customer.

The resulting content can not only focus on the employees who are learning but also on the content that is being taught. The "10 most important findings" from a seminar can result in an exciting blog post or ten short posts for social media.

D.

Products and services

Communicating its own products and services to the outside world is something that every company does anyway. Most output, however, is too self-centered, too promotional, and not exciting, varied, and humorous enough, and also not connected enough to benefits for the customer.

To say “We offer this and it‘s great” is definitely not creative enough for product news that should be distributed on various online channels. In the following, you will find a number of ideas on how you can turn your product information into many exciting contributions.

39. Products and services

🕐**$**

Even if your network doesn‘t appreciate being bombarded with product offers, nothing speaks against pointing these out in the form of posts from time to time. Especially, but not only, if you are new you should. But you will definitely find ideas below to make it more interesting for the target group.

40. “Making of” products and services

🕐**$**

For many of the products we buy or consume every day, we have never thought about how they are made and therefore often have no idea. „Making of“ content, which shows in detail and individual steps how a product is manufactured, or a service implemented, not only fills this knowledge gap but also produces a lot of diverse content for your digital channels.

The nice thing about it is that you can also stage the people in the production process, which makes the content even more interesting.

In this „making of“ you can also include those production steps that are upstream of your company. Where and how are e.g. the raw materials obtained for your products? What processing steps do other companies use, from which you buy parts or semi-finished products? Not only can a wonderful series of posts be made from this, but you can also involve your suppliers and join forces to achieve even more impact, reach, and attention online.

41. „Making of“ projects

🕐🕐**$**

Not only products and services that are produced repeatedly or in series can be documented as a „making of“. Even one-off products such as writing a book, or projects such as the construction or complete renovation of a building, can be wonderfully documented in a series of articles and posts.

42. Best-selling products

⏱**$**

The "employee of the month" idea discussed in an earlier section of the book can be applied to products in a very similar way. Why not choose a product of the week that is the best based on certain criteria? In the simplest case, it can be the best-selling. This idea for postings makes a lot of sense wherever there is a larger to very large range of products or, theoretically, range of services. The trade, for example, is ideal for this.

43. Make sums

⏱⏱**$**

Sometimes very exciting numbers come out when you change the way of viewing or counting you use. For example, a barber shop could calculate how many meters of beard the barber cut in a day, a week, or even a month. He could also set this sum in relation to a completely different quantity.

For example, the statement could then be, "We cut 1,350 meters of beards in April. If you piece the individual whiskers together, that would result in a distance that extends from here (location of the barber) to XYZ (insert city of choice)."

A baker could count the amount of raw material, a builder could count the stacked bricks. If you then implement the whole thing in a pictorial and humorous way, the result may be a post that amazes your readers.

44. Product extremes

⏱⏱**$**

You could also present your product range on the basis of its extremes and thus make a completely different and therefore varied product presentation. Which extremes, of course, depends entirely on the type of products that you manufacture or sell. The biggest, smallest, thickest, thinnest, fastest, slowest, cheapest, most expensive, oldest, or youngest; let your imagination run wild.

At Samsonite, the leading manufacturer of luggage for which I worked for many years, dealers regularly carried out stress tests (a person jumping on a suitcase) and photographed or even filmed it in order to communicate the message "the most stable suitcase" - an idea from the "product extremes" category.

45. Record attempts

⏱⏱⏱**$$**

You can also develop the idea with the product extremes and stage and document record attempts in connection with your products and services. For example:

- Crates of beer stacked on top of each other by a brewery to form a record-breaking pile.
- A massage studio which competes in a 24-hour massage marathon.
- A barber who does most haircuts non-stop.
- The speaker holding a speech marathon.

Such record attempts are ideal for live streaming on social media. Regardless of whether the record attempt succeeds or not, you will, in any case, create a lot of exciting and often humorous content. Of course, remember this is a content idea that involves significantly more effort and work, but that can be absolutely worth the effort.

46. Product in different places

⏱⏱**$**

Your products can also be shown in a wide variety of, ideally unusual, locations. This is particularly useful if humor plays an important role in your content. Combined with the right text, this can produce funny posts, for example:

- The book in the open fireplace, burning, “The hot new thriller.”
- The sunglasses frozen in the freezer, “Really cool.”

Sticking with this idea, you could also take a product with you when you travel and photograph it in front of well-known sights. But you don‘t have to travel far to get there. Especially if you are a local supplier, show your product in front of the town sign for every place in your catchment area. “Product XY today in Z.” For a manufacturer of teddy bears, dolls, or the like, it could be a very nice strategy to send teddy on trips in this way.

47. Products with different uses

⏱**$**

Products often have different uses from what they were originally intended. For example, scissors can be used to cut paper, fabric, or plastic wrap. Showing products in all their uses is OK, but usually not very exciting. However, it can be exciting and a real eye-catcher if you exaggerate the uses to the extreme.

Let‘s take something as simple like a pencil. What else can you use a pencil for besides writing, taken to extremes?

- cleaning ears
- puting up long hair
- hold small plants in place
- as a weapon for self-defense
- eat sushi

I believe you can think of 100 more uses for pencils. That would be enough material for a humorous series of posts entitled "101 things you can do with our pencils—but shouldn't necessarily do."

You could also involve your online contacts and fans and ask them to be creative and post photos that show how they use your pencils.

Under the title, "Will it blend?" (Https://www.youtube.com/watch?v=KWqw5SpITg8) blendtec, a manufacturer of high-performance mixers, has produced a series of videos that have made the brand and its mixers famous. In these videos, the brand's mixers successfully shred all sorts of things - golf balls, smartphones, beer mugs - there is hardly anything that can withstand these mixers.

48. Organize a photo / video contest with your product

🕐🕐🕐**$$**

When you use the above strategies your online contacts will become active themselves and post how they use your product. But, you also can ask people to do so. Organize a contest for your product. Depending on the product, these can be different types of use, locations, or variants for products with design options. For example:

- off-road vehicles in off-road use - the more extreme the better
- curling irons - the most creative hairstyles that customers make with the product
- materials - what creative and beautiful things can customers do from or with epoxy resin?

Bergzeit, a provider of hiking equipment, has called on website visitors in connection with the Corona curfew under the motto "Bergzeit at home" to send in photos showing them how they use the products at home. The result is a multitude of creative and humorous images and material for a huge number of posts.

49. Product reviews

🕓🕓**$**

Product reviews from customers and users can be used successfully as contributions e.g. distribute on social media. Not only do you use it to create additional, meaningful content, but also these advocates for your products and services are much more credible than if only you, as the seller, say good things about your products.

Reviews are all the better (provided, of course, that they are positive) if the reviewer is cited by name, even better with profession, place of residence, and maybe even a photo. This significantly adds to the credibility of the review.

Use tools and platforms like:

- Proven Expert
- Trusted Shops
- Google
- Facebook
- Ebay, Amazon, and other shops (if you offer your products there)

and encourage your customers to leave reviews.

Regardless of such rating platforms, you can, of course, also ask all your customers to give you written feedback or leave a review. For this to happen, it is important to include the question of the review as part of the post-purchase process in a standardized manner. But short video reviews from customers or attendees (if you‘re selling events) are absolutely feasible and make wonderful contributions to your online channels.

50. Product tests and comparisons

🕓🕓🕓**$$**

Product tests or comparisons are regularly carried out by institutions, website operators, or even professionally experienced bloggers. If your product is included in such a test and scores well, you should, of course, publish it on all your channels.

You can also carry out and document tests and comparisons yourself and use the results as a basis for postings. Good documentation and a high level of credibility are particularly crucial. In this context, reference should again be made to the example from blendtec that I mentioned earlier. These mixer tests alone ensured a huge range and quickly made the excellent product known.

E.

Customers

You should definitely include your customers in your content concept. As mentioned in a few of the ideas for content in the previous section, your customers can help you produce content for your digital channels in a number of ways. There are a few more ideas for doing this in this section.

51. Customer references

🕑🕑**$**

Testimonials from satisfied customers are a proven marketing tool. In the digital world, you have even more options than just offline, as follow:

- Obtain short, written statements from satisfied customers and publish them - ideally with a picture of the customer, their name and, if appropriate, their job, to increase the credibility of the statement.

- Produce a short video with a brief statement from a customer. This can be implemented easily and efficiently, especially in the context of events. There you can create several such video statements in a short time. In theory, your customers could also record reference statements on video and send them to you. Practice shows that it works more reliably when you take production into your own hands.

Obtaining meaningful and credible reference statements is not difficult in itself, but more a question of systematic implementation. If you incorporate the request for a reference statement into your post-purchase process as standard, you will receive more than enough positive statements that you can use for your online channels.

52. Interviews

🕑🕑**$**

Interview your customers on a topic related to your products and services. This is not about getting a customer review or positive feedback on your products. This type of interview is broader.

For example, a brick manufacturer could interview builders and ask them about mistakes they, or one of the service providers, have made in a construction project, and what they learned from them, without even mentioning their own products.

To ensure interviews do not just become “an uninteresting conversation,” it is vital to define the topic very precisely beforehand and to prepare exciting questions. The approximate duration should also be determined in advance.

Depending on the goal and channel, there can be very short interviews of just a few minutes or concepts in which interviews of an hour or more are conducted. There is no such thing as "too long" in this context, just "too uninteresting" or "too long" for a particular channel.

Germany's leading business magazine, Impulse, uses this strategy intensively to put customers in the foreground. They are interviewed on topics that are of interest to other customers and put online as a podcast. This podcast is also saved in video format and promoted via social media channels.

53. Tips, tricks, and hacks

🕐🕐$

Customers often use your products much more often and more intensively than you do and sometimes know more about them than the seller or manufacturer. It's amazing how many tips, tricks, and hacks exist on certain products and providers. For example, if you enter the search term "Ikea Hacks" on Google, more than 34 million results are displayed. In this case, it's often about what else you can do with Ikea furniture or how you can easily convert it and thus improve or expand its use.

But such tips, tricks and hacks can also cover other topics:

- Carry out small, simple repairs yourself,
- Tips for cleaning and care,
- Tips for faster, easier use,

to name just a few examples.

You can not only collect such tips, distribute them in your online channels and use them for your own content, but you can even actively request your customers and users (possibly in a competition) to send you tips or to post them on their own channels.

It makes sense to use your own hashtags for this. On Facebook, for example, a quick search for photos with the hashtag #ikeahacks will reveal a lot of pictures that have been posted by customers and users. You can also set up your own pin boards or even groups on platforms like Pinterest.

54. Customer Photos

🕐🕐$

Photos of satisfied, happy customers are of course the classic par excellence that you should definitely not be without.

- The proud car owner at the handover of his new vehicle
- The family in front of their new house (here, of course, there is also the idea

of documenting the whole process as a "Making of")

- The vacationers with a selfie in front of the beach hotel (which they post as agreed on the travel agency's Facebook page)
- Hairdressers could also do this after their work is done. The possibilities in this area are almost limitless.

55. Celebrity Photos

⏱⏱$

Do you have prominent customers? If so, then you should of course - without being intrusive - do everything you can to incorporate this into your content somehow. The simplest strategy is to take a picture of yourself with the celebrity or celebrities in or in front of your company and post it with a few lines of text.

This is traditionally often done by restaurateurs in particular. The walls of some hotels, restaurants and bars are full of such images, but mostly only analogue and therefore with a very low reach. If you already have images like this, the easiest and most obvious strategy is to digitize and post them. If you have a lot, make a series of them.

Not only does this strategy result in popular posts that can generate high reach. In addition, they also extremely enhance your image. Success rubs off. When you show up with celebrities, you will become prominent yourself over time. Due to this effect, many a restaurateur has become a celebrity himself and enjoys a higher VIP status than some of his prominent guests.

A small variant of this strategy is used by speakers, experts of all kinds, and people in art and culture. You show yourself - ideally captured in a photo - with celebrities without them being customers. Celebrities are approached at events and asked to take a selfie together. The wish is fulfilled again and again and the strategy "Show yourself to celebrities and you will become prominent yourself" definitely works.

Paul Misar, entrepreneur and real estate investor, pursues this strategy again and again and can be seen in photos with very well-known personalities (here with Richard Branson).

https://www.pinterest.at/pin/471963235929718491/

Paul Misar mit Richard Branson und Paul Misar
6. April 2014 ·

Hab Euch hier noch ein Foto von Richard Branson und mir unterschlagen - aufgenommen hinter der Bühne nach meinem und unmittelbar vor seinem Auftritt bei LIGHT THE FIRE - Woodstock für Unternehmer in Hamburg.

[redacted] und 19 weitere Personen

56. The most unusual Customer Requests or Inquiries

🕐🕐$

In some industries there are unusual or even curious customer requests. If this happens to you again and again, then you should collect them (usually anonymously) and use them on your online channels. This idea would also have potential for a series if you are frequently confronted with such customer requests.

57. Customer Complaints

🕐🕐$

One idea that takes a little courage and a lot of tact is to post complaints from customers. This is a good idea if the complaints are either funny and curious (without embarrassing the customer, of course), or if you are linking the complaint to a learning experience for your company and how that complaint helped you get better.

In this case, you can even go a step further and honor the customer as a "management consultant" and give him a prize for the "suggestion for improvement" of the month or week.

58. Say thank you

🕐🕐$

Even a simple thank you can be material for a post. You could use a social media post to thank the customers who bought from you today or this week or who made use of your service. This strategy would be perfectly conceivable for a car dealer, but I would definitely not recommend it to a doctor.

59. Before / After

🕐🕐$

So-called before / after photos are very popular and often very effective. Fitness trainers, nutritionists, hairdressers, barbers, car plumbers, gardeners, renovators, painters, style consultants, beauticians and cosmetic surgeons are just a few examples of professions that can and often use this strategy to create content.

There is little that is more convincing than photographic evidence (ideally combined with a statement by the customer, possibly also as a video) of how a positive service has had on a customer. Sometimes this idea can also be optimally combined with a "Making of" in order to create even more content from it.

Lukas Grigorescu, personal trainer and fitness expert (www.progressive-training.at), uses pictures like this to impressively demonstrate the effectiveness of his training methods.

https://bit.ly/30z9SY5

Progressive Personal Training ist hier: Progressive Personal Training.
6. Dezember 2019 · St. Pölten ·

Du möchtest wissen, wie man 50kg abnehmen kann und in die beste Form seines Lebens kommt?

Dann lies dir jetzt das Interview mit Gangolf:
https://progressive-training.at/ergebnisse/gangolf-pucher/

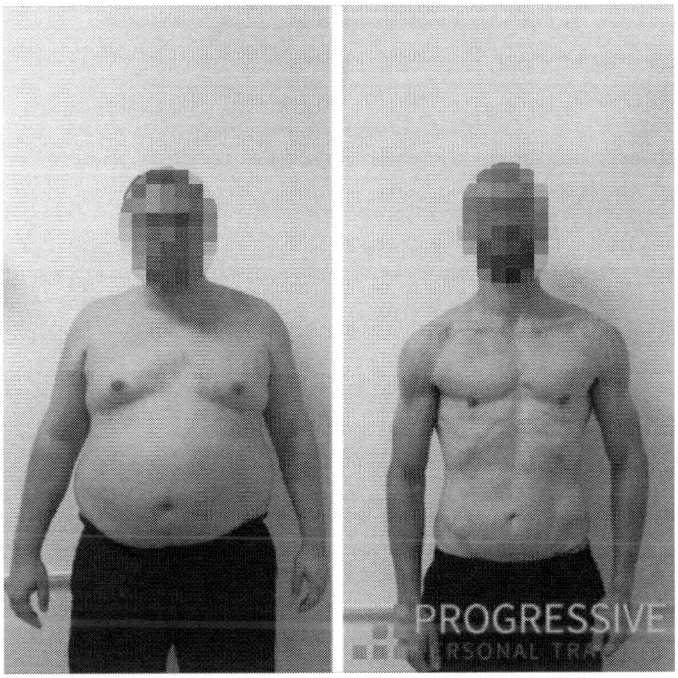

Du und 74 weitere Personen   11 Kommentare 3 Mal geteilt

60. Share Customer Posts

⏱$

You should have your customers on your online radar too. As mentioned earlier, Google Alerts is a tool to help you do this. But also in the social media it is recommended to like customer pages or to connect with customers and to like their posts again and again.

This ensures that you will be seeing them more often. You can also go a step further and share relevant contributions from your customers and thus create additional content for your channels. In addition, your customers will be happy if you help them expand their reach.

61. Customer of the Month

⏱⏱$

As with employees, there can also be a "customer of the month". The criteria according to which you choose this must be determined.

- A couple of ideas:
- The one who bought the most
- The one who was the first to buy a new product or service

- The one who was chosen by your employees as customer of the month in a secret ballot

- The one who was there most often (in restaurants, for example)

In any case, you should be very sensitive when making your selection. The other customers shouldn‘t feel left out or disadvantaged.

62. *New Customer of the Month*

⏱⏱**$**

In a slightly modified form, you could use the previous idea in such a way that you introduce all new customers or all new members (in a club, fitness center, etc.).

63. *Birthdays*

⏱**$**

Of course, customer birthdays can also be celebrated digitally if you know the dates. The social media, which reminds of the current birthdays every day, makes this idea a lot easier to implement.

In its simplest form, the congratulation is a short text post on the customer‘s social media profile or page.

But you could also make your own post on your profile in which you convey your congratulations to the customer and mark him so that he can also see it.

A warning at this point: There are a number of self-employed and entrepreneurs who use birthday wishes to hand over a “pseudo gift” (usually an e-book, a free initial consultation, etc.). In most cases, these gifts are just a sales activity and are often things that you always receive on the website of the well-wishers anyway. Accordingly, these gifts are often perceived negatively by the birthday child. “You notice the intention and are out of tune,” as the saying goes.

There is nothing to be said against gifts per se, but they should be real gifts. But better and easier to implement than real gifts are creative, humorous and, above all, very simple congratulations.

64. *Name Days*

⏱**$**

In the absence of birthday dates (or in addition to the birthday greeting), you can use name days to make creative posts with them. So, you could do a daily name tag post and tag all those people who have that name in your network.

Congratulations on your name day, perhaps even with a short info, where this name comes from and what he originally means are basically more exciting than birthday wishes, because hardly anyone congratulates for name day and you would stand out so much more.

65. T-shirt with Customer Logo

🕒🕒🕒$$

The American Jason Sadler has implemented a very unusual idea. For a whole year he wore a different T-shirt from a company every day and reported on social media about his campaign and everyday life. He even turned it into a business model by selling his days. The range effect was considerable. Details about this campaign and other, even more unusual ones by the author can be found in the book "Creativity for sale."

66. Personal customer information

🕒🕒$$

Without wanting to repeat everything, it should be pointed out that you can also transfer many of the ideas from the "personal" area to customers.

You can also ask customers ...

- for their preferences and what you dislike,
- for their favorite musicians and authors,
- for their favorite dishes,
- where they are going to for vacation

and much more. The best thing to do is to go through the list of content ideas in the "Personal" chapter and check the ideas there for transferability to your customers.

F.

Suppliers

For many companies, suppliers are extremely important partners when it comes to the success in business. Viewed in this way, it makes sense to include them in the creation of content. Firstly, this results in a lot of new, creative ideas and secondly, it makes you as a company likeable if you not only report about yourself and your own products and services, but also focus on others.

In principle, you can apply many, if not almost all of the ideas and strategies listed in other areas such as personal, employees, products and customers to your suppliers as well. You can go through these step by step and adopt those ideas that you think are also applicable to your suppliers and related partners (such as bankers, etc.).

67. Various Ideas for Suppliers

🕐🕐**$**

A few examples that might be particularly suitable for this (without wanting to repeat everything):

- Making of - include the parts of the production process that happen at your suppliers in your "making of."
- Introduce employees of the supplier, especially if they are an important contact person for you.
- Present (new) products and services from the supplier
- Birthdays and name days of the employees of the supplier
- Publish special services that the supplier has provided for your company (extremely quick delivery in a technical emergency, personal commitment, etc.)
- News about the supplier (e.g. awards and prizes that have been won)

Especially if your supplier is pursuing a similar strategy to yours in terms of content marketing and online presence, posts about suppliers can be very productive and successful. With a joint, coordinated effort, it is much easier to achieve significantly more attention and reach for both companies.

Health expert Bernadette Bruckner implemented a nice idea to present suppliers. She used the photo shooting to promote the photographer who put her in the picture as well. As a result of this post, a few more people wanted to book the photographer and thus shows how effective well-placed posts can be.

https://bit.ly/3kc3RZf

G.

Places, Rooms and Buildings

Not only where the business revolves around rooms - in the travel industry, in hotels, in architecture, in interior design, in the furniture industry or the construction industry, for example - but also in industries that have nothing to do with rooms per se , locations, rooms and buildings can serve as a basis and pool of ideas for online content. A few examples are given below.

It is of course important not to digress too far, but always to make sure that there is a recognizable and easily comprehensible connection between what you post and what you do for business.

68. Locations

🕐🕐**$**

You can create beautiful and personable content by bringing information about your location or locations (if you have several). A Berlin company that also has a branch in Vienna, one in Budapest and one in Milan can present the country, culture, festivals, people, sights, food and much more of the respective locations to the online network in the form of articles and article series.

But even if the Berlin company has no other locations, but customers in different areas or even countries, it can use Berlin and its particularities to create content for online channels.

69. The Company itself

🕐🕐**$**

The building or buildings in which the company is located, or the entire site, can be presented to potential readers and viewers. This can be your offices, production facilities or even warehouses. It's not about that it has to be something particularly worth seeing. Even "normal" offices can satisfy the curiosity of your online contacts and be seen with pleasure.

You can do this in the form of photos or film a tour of the company via video. Of course, this can be combined very well with a "making of" and the employees can be perfectly involved in such posts and articles.

70. Special Features of the Building

🕐🕐**$**

Does the building or the premises that you use for your company have any special features that are worth reporting? Such peculiarities could e.g. be:

- A special story
- Sustainable ecological energy supply
- A special design created by (famous) architects
- An unusual room concept

- Special materials that were used in the construction (e.g. only ecological, natural building materials)
- Rooms that are tailored to a new type of room use concept or a different way of working (meeting rooms with cushions on the floor instead of chairs, flexible workplaces / desk sharing, high tables for working, creative areas with Lego bricks, etc.)
- Any prizes won for the building
- Records like: the tallest office building in the city, the house with the lowest energy costs, etc.

Whatever your rooms and your building have to offer in this regard, you can report on it.

71. Removals, New Buildings and Renovations

⏱**$**

Moves to new premises or to new locations and renovations as well as new buildings are of course a must that you should report on. Larger projects in this context can also be processed as "making of." Before / after photos in the course of renovations of rooms and buildings are something that can be used very well for the one or the other post.

H.

Things

Things you report on can also be all sorts of things that are not directly related to your products, and private as well as professional. Above all, things get value for your content marketing if you manage to charge them emotionally. Usually this happens in connection with people in the form of the ideas and strategies that we discussed in the chapters on personal matters, customers, and employees.

72. The most important things in your office

🕐**$**

This could be a small series of funny or serious posts - it all depends on what kind of things it is. In many cases the funny or emotionally meaningful things for your posts yield more than the purely functional.

A good example of this is the NO button that is on my desk and does a good job in business.

73. Your favorite things

🕐**$**

This list of things doesn‘t have to be limited to your office, of course. Why not post a list of general favorite things from your private sphere too? You could also make these lists for several very different areas, such as:

- during sports
- during a meal
- for the holidays
- for the Christmas holidays
- for the weekend
- your hobbies
- your dog’s or cat‘s favorite things

The possibilities that arise from this are highly diverse.

74. Your customers, fans, and employees’ favorite things

🕐🕐**$**

You can implement the same concept of favorite things with your customers or employees. Every day a different person provides a list of their favorite things to post.

Roman Kmenta
21. Juni um 18:42 ·

Cooles Teil - gerade wiederentdeckt! - Eines der wichtigsten Dinge im Business! - Hör es dir an und du weißt warum 😉

26 10 Kommentare 1 Mal geteilt

https://bit.ly/33wFLCt

I.

Industry

The industry in which you operate contains a huge pool of information that you can convert into material for your content marketing. Not all industries are equally interesting for customers or other target groups such as future employees or the public. It is important to decide in advance whether your industry is suitable for this, and which industry information may be of interest.

75. News from the industry

🕐🕐$

The topic "news from the industry" could be dealt with in a regular series. To do this, you should determine in advance what types of news you want to report. Otherwise, it can get out of hand very quickly and then appear confused and without a concept. Focus on specific news such as:

- new products
- new technologies
- personnel changes in the industry.

That you would also be reporting about your competitors in the process may understandably seem strange at first. But if you take a closer look, that can make a lot of sense. You could position yourself as the expert who not only knows about their products and services, but also has more extensive knowledge than the other providers.

76. Industry Barometer

🕐🕐🕐$

The idea of an industry barometer builds on the previous one. It is, so to speak, a special variant of it. The aim is to regularly summarize certain key figures in a short form and to distribute them online in the form of tables, articles, or graphics (a highly recommended variant).

You can call up these key figures from official, existing figures or collect them yourself. Carrying out a regular survey on industry figures or topics, for example digitally automated, expends very little effort and, above all, brings content that is only available to you.

77. Interview influencers

🕐🕐🕐$

Most industries have influencers, people with a large reach, lots of fans and followers, and a lot of digital attention on their channels. These influencers are now getting paid well for their efforts to advertise a product or service.

But that's not all. There are still many influencers who earn their money in other ways and only use their reach for marketing purposes for their own products and services. They don't necessarily have to be the ones with 100,000 or millions of fans. Very often, people with a few thousand online contacts who are focused in a niche or a specific area can also have a great impact.Aside from paid advertising, you can join these influencers, in other words they can also be used in other ways. You can interview them on specific topics and post that interview online on your channels. There is a very good chance that the influencer will also share your post or article in their network.

As a tour operator, for example, you could do a series of articles on Asian travel destinations and interview a travel blogger about Vietnam for this purpose. They, in turn, earn their money by selling their books on the blog. They can include their latest book "Insider Travel Destinations in Vietnam" in the interview and benefit from the reach that the interview gives you on your channels. This is a practical example of this strategy where both of you win.

Whole books have been written on the subject of influencer marketing. It is sure to be an interesting topic that you could study further and make part of your company's content marketing strategy.

J.

Honors, Awards and Prizes

Honors and awards are interesting for your content marketing in two ways. On the one hand, those that you, your company or your products receive, and on the other, those that you give away.

78. Honors and awards you receive

⏱⏱**$**

Awards and prizes that you receive are always worth one, or even several, posts. Not only can you document the handover of the award and the award itself (if it is a physical thing) photographically or on video, but you can also turn it into a little story for your online channels. For example, first you post the work for which you are applying for the award, then the submission, then the fact that you have been nominated right up to the award ceremony and presentation.

If the handover takes place in the form of an event, you can get a lot more content out of your digital channels. Interviews with participants, a lot of photos of people, or a contribution about the other award winners. Everything is possible, but has to be well planned, both technically and in terms of content.

79. Honors and Awards you give

⏱⏱⏱**$$$**

Apart from the already mentioned employee-of-the-month or customer-of-the-month awards, which you can give and turn into content for your channels, there is the option of starting competitions or giving prizes. That can mean a lot more effort, but it also brings a lot more material.

The effort you have to put in to award your own prize pays off for you, especially if you don't only give this award once, but instead make it recurring onee.g. make it an annual event. Thanks to the experience gained, the organizational effort is reduced with each repetition and, at the same time, the awareness of the award increases and thus so do the benefits you can derive from it.

Photo: Trojan Horse Award – Prof. Anlanger (left; lender of the award) with Regina Kmenta

K.

Events

Just due to the large number of people, events are a very good vehicle to produce content for your digital channels. Many of the ideas listed in the other chapters can be implemented. Starting with a selfie of yourself at the event, through photos of other, interesting participants, to the funny table decorations which could be perfect as a snapshot for a post on Facebook or Instagram.

Go through these ideas in a structured way and check them for applicability in the context of the event you are attending or hosting. You will most certainly find what you are looking for and get a large number of ideas from it.

The following ideas are those that go beyond or complement what has already been written in the above chapters.

80. Event information

🕐🕐**$**

Producing content from events begins long before the event, for example in the form of event notices. But you don't have to limit yourself to the events you host or attend. In general, it can be events that are of interest to your target group, both your own and others.

Even the events of your competition are allowed. If your social media channels or website become the first point of contact for your target audience to find out about industry events, that is a very desirable effect.

You can even turn it into a real, fully-fledged event calendar that lists those events across all industries that are interesting from the perspective of your target group and not from the perspective of your product or service.

A fashion retailer could, for example, point out all local events which are about looking better, including fashion, shoes, hairstyle, cosmetics, tattoos, jewelry, glasses, weight loss etc. Everything is possible and allowed as long as it fits into a coherent overall concept and is interesting for your target audience.

81. Event reporting

🕐🕐**$$**

Event photos are so practical because there are potentially many people on them. If you not only post them, but also tag them (on Facebook, for example), you increase the chance of getting likes, comments, and shares. But be careful! Do this with a sure instinct. Not everyone likes this.

Especially if it is your own event, you should definitely not have to take all of the photos yourself. Since you are very likely to have a lot of other tasks to do with the event, photography would be neglected. In the end, you had a great event and almost no material from it for your channels. Of course, especially for larger events, hire photographers who have the task of capturing as many participants as possible and the most important activities. Nothing speaks against it, only it may be too little or too slow from the point of view of content creation.

If the event is important enough for you, assign a person to ensure that it is reported live during the event and that a lot of material is created from it. It's not just about photos, but also about text, video interviews, and much more. The technical quality is not decisive here. The slightly fuzzy snapshot that was created with a smartphone and immediately posted on Instagram can bring you a lot more than perfectly exposed and post-processed photos two days later.

So, it's more about digital reporting from the event than just resultant photos or a video. To do this, you need someone who is not only technically adept with pictures, videos, and text, but who can also approach people (for surveys, interviews, etc.), who is familiar with online channels, especially social media, and has immediate access to your channels.

82. Live streaming

🕐🕐**$**

A special version of event reporting is to stream the entire event live. You can do this on just one channel or on several at the same time. For example, it is conceivable to capture an overview of the entire event with a permanently installed camera, to stream it on another channel at the same time with a smartphone, and to simultaneously interact with the participants (conversations, interviews, etc.).

After the event, you can cut out and post parts of all the collected material, or create an event video that you can use for promotional purposes when the event is repeated (the next year, for example).

83. Your personal reporter

🕐🕐**$$$**

The American social media guru Gary Vaynerchuk goes one step further. He has his own 'reporter' who accompanies him every step of the way and constantly films and photographs him. This material is then edited graphically and textually by a content team and converted into contributions, often just as small bites and snippets, and distributed in the digital universe. The content recycling described above is carried out in its purest form. The result is an infinite number of snapshots through to long videos.

It is clear that not everyone can or chooses to pay for their own permanent reporter, and that this does not make sense for everyone. Still, the strategy of Garyvee (his social media stage name) is exciting enough to think about and use at least occasionally and in part for yourself.

84. Interviews with Speakers from Events

⏱⏱$

Interviewing presenters at events, preferably after the presentation because they are more relaxed, can be a very good thing if it thematically fits your content marketing goals. A lot of money is often spent so that experts or celebrities appear at events and speak there. However, it can then be very easy and even free to win them over for an interview. It may be a little more difficult with big celebrities and VIPs, but, in my experience, experts like to give interviews because it increases their own reach. Make sure to mark the interviewees when you publish the interview online. They will usually be happy to help you disseminate the interview by distributing it through their own channels.

At congresses or trade fairs, where there are usually a large number of lectures, you can turn them into a series with little effort. It is important that you prepare the interview, its planned duration and, most importantly, the questions you will ask.

By the way, you should also clarify beforehand with the organizer that they do not disapprove of your planned interviews. Of course, if you are concerned that the promoter could refuse your plan, you can do it quietly, but not without first checking how high is the risk that you could be taking.

85. Interviews with event participants

⏱⏱$

You can also interview event participants. Here, it is even more important that you come up with a concept for these interviews, which will often be very short and only consist of one to three questions. The concept can be for example, that you ask a single question, appropriate to the event and your goals, but address it to as many event participants as possible.

Especially when it comes to interviews with many participants, you should also clarify beforehand what data protection law needs to be observed. Otherwise, what was said about the previous point applies here, especially when it comes to tagging / marking the interviewees.

86. The best ideas or quotes from events

⏱$

A lot of content is produced at larger events with, often, many speakers, but also as part of a seminar that lasts one or two days. Another possibility for you to turn it into something for your channels is to collect and post the best ideas or quotations from the lectures and the seminar content in the form of short text contributions. The combination with a snapshot of a presentation slide is often very easy to do.

The other things mentioned in the previous points also apply here.

87. Review of the event

⏱⏱$

From the material that you gathered by implementing the previous ideas, you can create a summary and use it to look back at the event. This can be in the form of a longer blog post or a video (which may be a little more effort).

88. Flash mobs

⏱⏱⏱$$

Flash mobs offer a wide range of possibilities to draw attention to certain topics. If you are the organizer of a flash mob yourself, this may involve more effort for you, depending on the type of implementation. A flash mob does not always have to be elaborate, depending on the goal and topic.

The balcony singing often practiced during the corona crisis is also a kind of flash mob. The success was resounding. Laypeople, professionals, and many in between took part to draw attention to the loneliness associated with the exit restrictions. This has resulted in a large number of videos and posts on YouTube and all sorts of social media channels.

How could you use it for your own purposes, you might ask? A music school could post and distribute these contributions in connection with its own offer, according to the motto: "So that you are better prepared for the next crisis."

Of course, there is a lot more to be said and taken into account when it comes to staging flash mobs. However, that would go beyond the scope of this book. So, I just want to leave your own flash mob as an idea here.

Another source for your content marketing that is much easier to use can be flash mobs hosted by others. You can use these, similar to the events mentioned above, to produce a lot of content for your channels. The challenge for you will be to find a flash mob that thematically fits your goals.

89. Demonstrations

🕐🕐🕐**$$**

Demonstrations can also be used very well for your online marketing. They are another facet of the idea of doing something in the offline world and then using it in the online world. Demonstrations are much easier to carry out than many may think. You need a suitable hook for it, at least a few co-demonstrators, and you have to have the action approved by the police, which is surprisingly easy and unbureaucratic, especially if the action does not appear dangerous in any way.

On the occasion of Black Friday, I myself have organized demos several times in Austria and Germany to demonstrate against the rampant discount offers and cheap prices. During the demonstration, we, as a small group, carried a coffin in the form of a corpse procession through the shopping streets of Vienna and Cologne. The high value, the quality, the sustainability, and the economic efficiency were symbolically carried to the grave. The media response, both on and offline, was high. And, of course, we produced a lot of photos, videos, and texts from them ourselves.

Demo with coffin - Roman Kmenta - Photo: Mario Pernkopf

L.

Animals and Nature

Animal posts are one of the most popular and shared themes online. Posts with particularly cute and cuddly animals, baby animals, or videos of animals that exhibit strange or funny behaviors keep going viral in the online world and create huge reach in the millions.

For that reason alone, it makes a lot of sense to deal with the topic of animals and nature in the context of your content marketing, especially if the connection to your service or product does not exist at first glance.

90. Animals in general

⏱$

Animal photos, especially funny and cute ones, are always worth a post if you can get them connected to your business. With suppliers of pet food and products for pet owners, this is easy, and this strategy is a must. The simplest approach in this case is to depict the animal using their products. But animal photos can also be used in completely different industries and areas, such as:

- A hiking hotel could, for example, post photos of animals from the local mountains as a series of articles.
- A car tire manufacturer could use animal photos to draw attention to the particularly short braking distance of its products by showing photos of animals whose lives car drivers save when they use their tires.
- The office animal - the office dog, goldfish, or parrot can become a real social media star.

91. Animals in disguise

⏱⏱$

Animals in disguise are a specific section of animal photos. Of course, one could argue about whether it is morally okay to put animals in funny disguises and thus expose them to ridicule. You have to decide with a sure instinct whether this strategy is OK for you and, above all, for your target group, or whether it already exceeds the limits of decency. This strategy always produces entertaining photos and funny videos.

The views of such videos often run into the millions. Simply enter “animals disguise” in the search field on YouTube and you will find a large number of videos with high coverage.

92. Nature

🕐🕐$

Photos of beautiful or interesting things in nature (landscapes, trees, flowers, etc.) are not always easy to link to every topic, but they are gladly seen and liked. Online users really like natural beauty. Using this as part of the content marketing strategy is pretty easy for anything that has to do with travel, vacations, and holidays.

Even a food manufacturer can incorporate the plants and the areas where they are grown into their contributions and posts. If your company is located in a scenic or at least interesting area, you can certainly incorporate photos of it into your digital content. Let your creativity take over your mind and body. It will not always be possible to find meaningful connections, but significantly more often than one would think at first glance.

M.

Occasions

In this context, occasions primarily mean recurring festivals and holidays. These have the huge advantage for your content planning that they take place every year or even several times a year. This makes them very easy to plan for your content creation. Often you can repeat the same online activities and even posts every year, at least for a while.

93. Classic occasions and holidays

🕑🕑**$**

Think about how you can use the classic occasions related to content for your online channels. These occasions are mainly:

- Christmas
- Mother's Day
- Father's Day
- End of school
- Start of school
- Easter
- Pentecost
- New Year's Eve
- Thanksgiving
- Carnival
- Valentine's Day
- Halloween.

If you sell flowers or make cosmetics it's simple, but how do your products fit Mother's Day if you are a car dealer, builder, or do cleaning services? It doesn't just have to be consumer products or services for which you create Mother's Day material. Admittedly, it is usually easier to find and create suitable content for the B2C area. If only because what is offered can often immediately be a Mother's Day present.

However, areas that have nothing to do with end users can also be linked to such occasions, also taking into account the other strategies mentioned (such as employees, animals, etc.). Here's a somewhat extreme example of this, just to show what would be possible—the guys from the foundry of a metalworking company, often strong, hard-working, seasoned men in heavy work clothes, could congratulate their mothers on Mother's Day via social media, either individually as a small series (with a flower in their hand), or as a group with a group photo in front of the furnace with glowing metal. It is precisely this extreme contrast that can make such posts eye-catching and, therefore, very successful.

Note that you have to combine this with a suitable message with which you also make a contribution to achieving your content marketing goals with such a post. It is similar for all other classic occasions.

94. Special days and occasions

Many people are surprised how many local or regional holidays there are. Many of these days have a very serious background (the end of a war, the anniversary of an uprising, etc.) and can, if they fit your company or your goals, serve as a basis for contributions and posts.

However, many of these holidays fall into the category "strange and funny" and may stimulate your imagination.

Here are a couple of examples:

- Day of the Straw (January 3rd)
- World Milk Day (June 1st)
- Crossing Day (September 1st)
- Handbag Day (October 10th)
- Hug a Bear Day (November 7th)

A very extensive list of such curious holidays can be found at https://www.timeanddate.com/holidays/fun/. The backgrounds and origins of these holidays are explained, which will help you to find ideas for good online content. An even more detailed list of days of remembrance and action, which is not limited to curious holidays but includes all days of this type, can be found on Wikipedia at https://bit.ly/389HbVL.

When in need of ideas, search for these terms on social media. If, for example, you enter World Milk Day or #worldmilkday on Twitter, you will find an incredible variety, not only of private posts but also of companies that use this special day as an opportunity to create content. The diversity of companies and organizations is astonishing.

The list is endless. If all these organizations can think of suitable content for World Milk Day, then the chances are very high that you will also have inspiration.

The Black Friday demo mentioned in the chapter about events, which I have already held several times, is also an example of how you can use such occasions for yourself.

95. Special hashtags for occasions

⏱$

Hashtags go particularly well with the topic of special days and occasions, so here's a brief reference.. When using such occasions for your content marketing, or, in fact, any topic, you should use relevant hashtags such as #mothersday #blackfriday or #worldmilkday. This increases your reach and visibility in the digital jungle.

There are basically two options:

- Use existing, often widespread hashtags, such as e.g. #valentinesday, #christmas or #karneval—which is recommended in any case
- Create your own hashtags such as #grow (one of my book titles). The latter can include your message, your company name, a product name—so-called brand or branding hashtags—or the name of a campaign you initiated.

N.

Impulses

In the following, impulses are to be understood as everything that is primarily intended to stimulate thought. Often these are very small, short contributions. But longer articles can also be created from them.

96. Quotes

⏱$

Quotes are a classic in this field. Quotes stimulate thought and provide courage and energy. The right quote in the right place can often go a long way. That‘s probably one of the reasons why quotes are still popularly liked and shared. Quotes work best online if they are graphically beautiful or attractively presented.

If quotes are a path you want to take when creating online content, the best thing to do is to make a list of the quotes that fit your goals and have them graphically processed in larger quantities, like a few hundred. Then you have the same amount of material for posts. This approach works particularly well with quotes because there are a large number of online database sources of quotes and collections of quotes that make content creation much easier.

97. Claim the opposite

⏱⏱$

If you oppose the opinion and point of view of the general public in a contribution or post, you will get attention at least once. A contribution entitled “Five reasons why we need more refugees” would at least attract attention and stimulate discussion. Of course, once again there is the challenge of justifying the controversial tag and linking it to your topic.

There are several ways to create ideas for this. Here are just two of them:

Topics that concern the public and media

You can compile a collection of topics that are receiving a lot of media attention, like the refugee crisis, the corona crisis, global warming, Brexit, or even electric mobility. You formulate statements on these topics that contradict the general opinion represented by the major media or broad sections of the population. Then you formulate a counter statement for each of these statements to then think about how you can bring them into a meaningful connection with your business.

If you can‘t find a meaningful connection a humorous one could work. But, be careful! The big issues are often crises and disasters. Opinions to the contrary must therefore be formulated and explained with a great deal of sensitivity. Even a humorous contribution can quickly turn into the opposite and catch the eye.

Topics related to your business

The second variant is the simpler one. In principle, the procedure is the same, except that you start with topics that are already closely related to your business or to the industry. Often these are topics that may not be of interest to the general public but that interest your target audience strongly. For example, if you, as a gardener, say, "Stop watering your plants" or, as a doctor, write, "Why vegetables are bad for your health" or even more pointedly use the title "Killer vegetables," that is definitely an eye-catcher and, with content that justifies the thesis well, a contribution that can achieve greater reach.

If that seems too far-fetched to you, it isn't. The American physician Steven R. Gundry wrote a book entitled "Bad Vegetables - How Healthy Foods Make Us Sick," which became a bestseller.

Photo: Oliver Reetz

Provoke

By taking an opposite view, you are provoking some members of your digital network. You can, of course, take this one step further by simply provoking without concrete content, as publisher Julien Backhaus did in his "Stinkefinger-Post."

https://bit.ly/30A3GiF

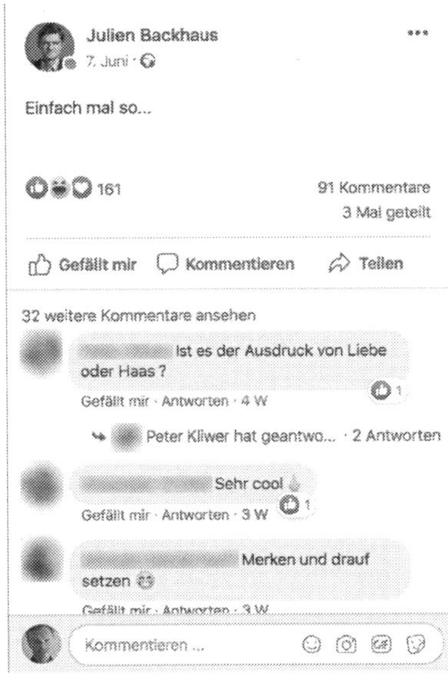

98. Critical reactions to third party content

🕐🕐$

Of course, don't just claim an opposite view in your article or post. You can also post your counter statement as a comment on a post that states mainstream opinion and thus the opposite of what you are saying.

99. What-if posts

🕐🕐$

You can set impulses and stimulate thought by asking a question with the structure "What if ..." in a post, or by sketching a relevant scenario.

- What if we had an unconditional basic income, how would it change your life?
- What if you were Federal Chancellor for a day and could pass a new law, what would it be?
- What if there was no more meat to eat from now on, what would that change for you?

Posts of this kind will often get higher interaction rates, especially more comments. There are no limits to your imagination. After looking at these hypothetical questions, you can literally make anything possible.

100. Predictions

🕐🕐$

There are experts whose business it is to predict the future or take a look at possible future developments. But, why should such content only be reserved for these few experts? Who would know better about trends and developments in a particular industry than someone who works in this industry?

So why not take a look into the future yourself? Become a trend researcher on your own behalf. Present possible future developments, products, and services. Of course, you don't know whether this will become reality, but neither do futurologists. So why not think about possible futures together with your digital contacts.

You could do this in a number of ways, such as:

- 10 theses on the future of the industry (a series of articles)
- 10 products that will be part of everyday life in 10 years
- The hottest trends in digitalization in tourism

And if your predictions or scenarios don't come true, no problem. First, all experts are also regularly wrong, sometimes completely. And second, it can still be very stimulating and reach-enhancing to discuss hypotheses about the future together.

101. Look back

⏱$

Not only looking into the crystal ball of the future can be productive for you, retrospectives can also result in interesting content for your digital channels, where you can bring back revised posts or simply repost something. If you posted something five years ago it can basically be re-posted unchanged without hesitation if the tag is right.

Either the content is still up to date, or—and this always works—you post such posts under tags like:

- There was once ...
- Five years ago today ...
- Can you remember ...
- What has changed in the last 30 years
- Our bestsellers 20 years ago

Experience shows that a little nostalgia inspires many people. Photos with music cassettes from the 70s regularly receive many likes and shares from people who remember their youth, while younger followers sometimes wonder what it is supposed to be, or what it is all about.

Of course, if necessary, a lot more can be made of the idea, as shown by waves that regularly go through the various social media platforms. For example, someone posts a youth photo of themselves. Many others find the idea so good that they are happy to participate.

The connection with the idea of holding contests or competitions can also result in interesting content.

0.

Information, interesting facts, and education

Technical, factual information makes up a huge portion of online content. This information can be found primarily in written form and, in some cases, videos. These are partially supplemented by detailed graphics.

While it is the case with many of the other ideas already discussed that you may or may not use them for your content strategy, there are hardly any entities that should or can do without well-founded articles. Getting active in this area is a must.

102. Technical articles

🕐🕐🕐**$**

Technical articles, even more extensive ones, mostly as blog or video, are a standard form of content in most areas. Of course, these are associated with more effort in research and creation. However, a lot of content recycling can be done with such longer contributions. A large blog post or video can be used to create many smaller posts and snippets of content with little effort.

103. Articles in the print media

🕐**$**

If you have published an article in a traditional print medium, i.e. a newspaper or magazine, or if such an article was published about you, then digitize it by scanning it in or photographing it and then posting it. This approach not only brings you additional, valuable content, but also makes a massive contribution to building your credibility and your expert status (more ideas on this later). The credibility—depending on the medium—is still felt to be greater with offline media than with online. It is easier to appear anywhere online than to be printed offline.

104. Podcasts on non-podcast channels

🕐**$**

Another channel that contains a lot of specialist content with heavy content is podcasts. However, you can also post a specialist article that you have published as a podcast or a podcast interview that was conducted with you on a third-party podcast on other channels.

You should provide the podcast with a background image and also to save it as a video. Then you can publish it on all channels where pure audio files are not possible - on YouTube, Facebook, and LinkedIn, for example. The additional effort for this is almost zero, as the software for creating or editing podcasts automatically does this with just one click.

105. Interesting and fun facts

⏱$

True to the motto “Did you know that ...” you can post amazing facts that are worth knowing. This can often be done in brief. If the meaning of a fact is low, but the fact is still interesting, astonishing, or entertaining, one speaks of so-called fun facts. These—best shown as a picture—are liked and shared with pleasure. The reach of such posts is, sometimes regrettably, often much higher than with substantial and serious posts.

To create fun facts in your business or industry, it can be helpful to think about all possible dimensions and their extremes, or to research them.

If someone manufactures and sells bicycles, then fun facts could be answers to questions such as the following (the difference between fun facts and normal information is fluid):

- When was the first bike built?
- Where was the first bike made?
- Who invented the bicycle?
- How old is the oldest bike?
- By what strange coincidence was the wheel invented (if there was one)?
- How far does a professional cyclist get with just one step on the pedals?
- How often would you have to pedal to get around the world?

What other interesting numbers, data, and facts are there that hardly anyone wants to know, but which are interesting for many?

106. News and trends

⏱⏱$

What‘s on the news right now? Which topics or which people? Every day topics move the masses that you can attach yourself to with your post. You do not have to claim the opposite—as described in the “Impulses” chapter—you can use the current topics in such a way that you analyze, explain, and comment, and thus establish a reference to your topics. Here, too, the use of the associated popular hashtags is particularly important in order to get more visibility and reach.

Check the currently most important topics on Twitter or Google Trends regularly and check them for usability for your marketing.

107. “How to” content

🕐🕐$

You can fill your digital channels with “how to” content alone, if you want. “How to” content is understood to mean all the content that explains how something works. This type of content is a source of popular and widely consumed content in almost all areas of life and business.

A couple of examples:

- E-mail marketing software manufacturer uses videos to explain how the individual functions of his software can best be used.
- A meat producer gives video grilling lessons, perhaps as a joint venture with a manufacturer of grills.
- A tile manufacturer or hardware store shows customers by video or a detailed description, which is supplemented with photos and graphics, how tiles are laid in which area.

What “How does it work?” questions can you answer for your customers?

108. Lists of ideas

🕐🕐$

The book you are reading contains a long list of ideas, apart from the first part, which covers certain basics. You can also use such lists of ideas very well for blog posts and then break them down into individual posts for your social media channels. If you also present the ideas as a picture or graphic, this is even better for your visibility. Content recycling is back in fashion too.

Here’s a separate example of this. I have compiled over 300 examples of possible unique selling points in a very long blog post and then turned them into a book - entirely in line with the idea of content recycling. This book, which you are currently holding in your hands, also emerged from a collection of ideas for a blog post.

109. Answer questions from the community

🕐🕐$

Many podcasts are based on the concept of answering questions from the community and making content from them. This strategy is not reserved for podcasts alone, although it is often found there. What questions do you get asked by your customers, users, and contacts on a regular basis, the answers of which may be interesting enough for others?

Ask your employees if you need answers to questions that they face every day. Using answers to such questions as social media posts or for podcast episodes has the additional advantage that you are asked these questions less often. This means you save time.

If you have too few or no questions from customers or contacts, turn them into posts in which you ask your contacts what questions they have.

110. Individual consultations

🕐🕐$

An extreme way of answering questions from the community is to give these answers in the form of one-on-one advice. The customer or prospect asks you their question or questions. You answer this in the form of a consultation or coaching conversation, depending on the industry, and record this consultation as a video. You can automatically generate the audio file for the podcast from it. Alternatively, you could even hold these consultations as part of a live video session.

111. FAQ / SAQ

🕐🕐$

FAQ (frequently asked questions) are questions that you are asked often in connection with your business. These can also be supplemented with SAQ (should ask questions), i.e. those that are not asked often, but should be. The difference is not really relevant in the end. Subpages and lists with FAQs can often be found on websites, but these are rarely used actively to make posts and contributions.

This strategy is about creating a comprehensive FAQ questionnaire and promoting it. This approach can be seamlessly linked to the two previous ideas. If you write this content in such a way that it can be found more easily by Google and you thus appear high in the results list of a Google search, you benefit from it even more.

112. Definition and explanation of technical terms - glossary

🕐🕐$

The idea of creating a glossary—a definition and explanation of technical terms that is as comprehensive as possible—on your website goes in a similar direction. First, something like this is very useful as a reference work, not only for customers, but also for your new employees. Second, you can also use it to regain reach and visibility via Google search.

Third, you can explain every single technical term in the form of a post and thus create a lot of material for your digital channels.

You could even turn it into a quiz if you're in an industry that has many very specialist terms. This is often the case with technical products and services, but a psychologist or therapist could also use this strategy wonderfully. For example, "do you know what 'transmission and counter-transmission' mean in the therapeutic area and what they may have to do with you?"

113. Analyses of companies

🕐🕐**$**

In some industries, analyses are the perfect strategy for creating meaningful and welcome content. In principle, everything can be analyzed, including products, services, websites, CI, graphics, behavior, people, clothing, vehicles, etc. What you analyze depends, above all, on what you sell.

These can be things from customers, which, of course, should be discussed with them, or things from non-customers.

Here are a couple of examples:

- A web designer analyzes a website both technically and in terms of design and points out the strengths, weaknesses, and potential for improvement.
- A style consultant analyzes a person and their outfit and gives tips on what they should and should not do.
- A construction specialist analyzes a new building or renovation project and shares things that have been solved well along with defects and weak points.

Analyses can be used primarily in areas where complex products or services are involved. The analysis of a glass of water is also feasible, but it is likely to generate less interest.

Although it's not that you can't use this idea for glasses. A comparative analysis of special wine glasses, carried out by a sommelier, can arouse great interest among wine drinkers and connoisseurs.

Customer acquisition analyses

On an additional note. sometimes such analyses are also used to win customers. In my experience, this is a good idea if this has been discussed with the potential customer and commissioned by them (even if you carry out the analysis free of charge).

Sending unsolicited analyses to potential customers in order to sell them your product or service is often not well received. The recipient could see this as unsolicited criticism of themselves and their previous decisions and, for that reason alone, they refuse any further contact. If you formulate the analysis very gently and in a well-meaning manner, such as the optimization ideas you have for the client, it will work better.

114. Case studies

⏱⏱⏱$

The difference between a detailed analysis and a case study is fluid. Case studies are often more comprehensive and detailed, sometimes so detailed that they are even published as a book. There is usually a time or chronological sequence in a case study, while an analysis is usually a snapshot. An analysis of the current situation could, however, serve as a starting point for a case study.

To put it simply, a short case study could be structured and prepared as follows:

1. What is the initial situation, what is the current situation? What are the strengths and pluses? What are the problems, obstacles and potentials?
2. What was changed / implemented / done - ideally with the help of your products or services?
3. What was the result? What worked, why, and what didn't? What learning experiences could be drawn from it?Case studies can be implemented both in written form supported by graphics and images and as video, especially in the form of an interview with the customer. Due to its size alone, a case study is also perfect for making many small pieces of content or bits that explain the development or story step by step.

115. The biggest mistakes

⏱⏱$

Of course, mistakes are often discussed in case studies. But mistakes and failures hold much more potential for your content creation than just being marginal notes in a post. You can focus on mistakes and make them the stars of your content. This type of view has seen a significant upswing in recent years.

There are entire books that deal only with the mistakes of, usually famous, personalities or companies and what can be learned from them. Even failure conferences and lecture series that focus on failures have been, and are being, held. Failure has lost its negative image in recent years and has emerged from the shadow of its existence.

So why not collect mistakes and use them to make content for your online marketing? It doesn't have to be only your own. Using the mistakes of others is far less painful and costly.

Ask your employees, suppliers, customers, and online contacts about mistakes they have made or that they know are widespread and turn them into a series of articles with a title like "The biggest mistakes," "The most expensive mistakes," or "The most common mistakes."

116. Behind the scenes

🕐🕐$

A variant of the „Making of" mentioned several times above is the idea of letting your contacts take a look behind the scenes, for example, theater or film productions lends themselves to this approach. You need to consider how far this strategy can be productive in your business.

However, in principle a "behind the scenes" view is possible pretty much everywhere. A farmer—there are more progressive farmers present on online channels than you might think—could talk about his daily work on the farm. A lawyer who often works in court could provide careful and discreet glimpses behind the scenes of everyday court life, and a speaker could cover all the invisible activities in the lecture business.

117. Recordings of Presentations

🕐🕐$

Do you hold public presentations or lectures? If so, the content could be of interest to your digital target audience You could record these on video and then distribute them, either whole or in parts, via your digital channels. Alternatively, or as a supplement, you could also convert the set of slides that you use for your presentation into an automatic slideshow and turn it into a video.

It doesn't have to be your own presentations either. Those of employees or external speakers, with their permission, can be used for the strategy.

118. Present information graphically

🕐🕐$

The subject of graphics, especially infographics, was briefly addressed in the first part of the book. But infographics are not just a form of media representation, you can also use infographics as a strategy. Infographics, to make the term more tangible, are graphic representations that show or explain a lot of information as clearly as possible in a graphic.

These can be from simple pie and bar charts to very elaborate and sometimes complex flowcharts that depict processes. In addition to graphic elements, most infographics also contain many numbers and texts. An organization chart e.g. viewed in this way is of course also an infographic.

Infographics have the advantage that information presented in this form is more readily consumed and absorbed by viewers. It is more effortless to look at a graphic than to read potentially lengthy text.

Of course, as already mentioned, you can use infographics to represent one or the other content, but if you want to use infographics as a real strategy you need to be more systematic.

As a first step it is advisable to use the heavy and substantial content, and possibly also the fun facts described above, that you already have or want to create as a basis, and to mark those parts that you represent as an infographic. Similar to quotations, for example, it is advisable to hire a graphic artist who has experience with infographics for the implementation and to have a whole series of such graphics created ahead of time. This type of batch processing reduces the overall overhead.

When creating infographics, you have to be aware that not every format can be represented well in every channel. On Instagram, for example, your options are limited by the standard square shape of the picture posts. You can also post pictures in portrait or landscape format, but then you have to live with a white border. The fact that Instagram is likely to be consumed more than some of the other channels on mobile devices with smaller screens also affects the way your graphics are displayed. Too much information in a graphic with lots of numbers and small text makes little sense there.

The strategy of packing information in graphically beautifully designed, clear, and understandable explanatory diagrams is highlyrecommended. You will get a lot of attention and more likes than for other forms of presentation of the same information. Graphics of this kind are usually shared with pleasure and often.

119. Industry myths

🕐🕐**$$**

In many industries and for many products well known or popular myths have been passed down over a long period of time, often generations, that are sometimes no longer true. If you run your business in an area where such myths exist, you can use this as the basis for a series of articles and posts.

You can list these myths, shed light on their origins, explain why they are not correct, and reveal the truth about them. For example, if nutrition is your topic you could do a series of posts where you dispel the following myths:

- Coffee dehydrates the body
- Cola and pretzel sticks help with diarrhea
- Chocolate makes you happy
- Too much beer causes a beer belly
- You should drink three liters of water a day.

These are just a few of the nutritional myths that you could blog about. You could also easily turn it into a series of great, short text posts with pictures.

The same concept could be used for health, the body, weather, individual countries e.g. myths about America for a travel agency or a tour operator, psychology, environmental protection, and many more. Are there any myths in your industry?

120. Checklists

🕐🕐$

Information that you already have as content, for example as a blog post, can also be used to prepare a checklist and make it accessible to your audience. This is easy and makes a lot of sense. Apart from the fact that such checklists can be created quickly and easily and are very helpful for and acceptable to your target audience, you can also use them as an exchange object for your contacts' e-mail addresses.

121. Tests and self-checks

🕐🕐$

Tests, self-checks, and checks are widespread and popular, and not just in the weekend newspapers. People are interested in learning more about themselves, the people they surround themselves with, or their company. This is not about detailed analysis, although you could offer these for a fee anyway, but about short, small, simple tests and checks that can be done quickly. If they take too long, the interest in filling them out may decrease.

If your self-check has a "psychological" touch or is even a well-founded, psychological test, it will meet with interest from many people. But also, short tests with which you can analyze the status quo of a company or person with regards to a certain topic and learn something new are gladly accepted.

Just like checklists, tests and self-checks can also be used to collect the email addresses of potential customers and interested parties.

If you take this strategy one step further, you can create even more interesting content with it. The self-checks do not have to be available for download but can be implemented in the form of an online questionnaire. In this way, you can summarize and evaluate the results of many test participants. This gives you a lot of often very exciting numbers and data that you can convert into new and interesting content.

122. Helpful online tools

🕐$

The basic idea of content marketing is to be helpful and useful to your contacts. A very good way of providing support for your target audience is to bring information about technical tools, both paid and, especially, free, that make it easier for you to run your business.

That can be, for example, graphic tools, email marketing software, or computers and calculators of all kinds.

https://www.romankmenta.com/price-promotion-calculator/

romanKmenta

Price promotion calculator

This calculator answers the following question: "By how much do I have to sell more or less, if I increase or decrease the price in order to achieve the same contribution margin?"

	old values	new values
Selling price	19,00	18,00
Price change	-	-5,3%
Purchasing price / Manufacturing costs	13,00	13,00
Units	100,00	120,00
Change units	-	20,0%
Contribution margin per piece	6,00	5,00
Total contribution margin	600,00	600,00

123. Explanation of online tools

🕐🕐$

If you want to dig deeper into the tool strategy you can also explain the tools that you introduce. This can go as far as recording training videos for individual tools in a "how to" style and posting them online. The question of how deep you dive into this strategy is closely related to which business you are in and how your business model works.

If you are a service company and offer advice related to these tools, then such "training videos" can still be a free offer for your target group, and an online video course is already a paid product. Of course, you have to decide in each individual case where the line between free content and paid product lies.

124. Comparisons of different tools

🕐🕐$

Another idea based on the tool theme is to make professional comparisons between tools to build your content, rather than just recommending individual ones. It could be real product tests in which you test the different tools, for example, ten different webinar platforms, and compare them in a structured way divided into different functional or application areas. Some website operators do only this as a business model.

125. Tips and comparisons for physical products

⏱⏱$

Everything that has been said in the last few points about online tools can also be implemented for offline tools or products. You can introduce and recommend individual tools, create videos to demonstrate how to use them optimally, and perform comparative tests between them.

Especially in the technical area there is always something new to report, show, and demonstrate. Show some equipment, demonstrate how it can be combined, and where it is best used. In this way, you will also build up expert status in this area.

At a time when we are constantly scrambling to the limit of technological overstrain due to regular technical innovations, we greatly appreciate people or companies who can explain to us simply how we can handle all these things or all this software, and we thank them with likes, comments, and shares.

126. Helpful pages

⏱$

Not only tools and products can be of interest to your contacts, but also certain pages that offer a lot of helpful information on a certain topic. Where can you send your contacts when it comes to topic X? This can be entire pages, but also individual blog posts or lists. Let the website operator or blogger know and they will probably be happy to help you to get an even wider reach and visibility.

127. Free

⏱$

You can also focus your posts on collecting useful but free content and recommending or offering it to your audience. Often these are books, e-books, and tools that are offered free of charge. These can be your own offers, but you can also use other offers that are helpful to your target audience. In this case you have the additional advantage that the provider of the free content will normally be happy to support you in gaining reach.

A variant of this is to do a freebie parade together with colleagues or clients. You summarize all the free offers on one page. This can now be easily shared and distributed by all participants. This significantly increases the scope of this idea.

P.

Content of others

So far, the talk has mostly been of ideas and strategies in which you create or produce content yourself, but that doesn't always have to be the case. In addition to the previously explained ideas, let's shed light on some possibilities for incorporating third-party content into your content strategy.

128. Share foreign contributions

⏱$

Contributions from others, especially the media, that fit your topic can be used well to create new content for your posts. In the simplest case, you share them on your channels and provide a suitable comment on your part. You will find what you are looking for in a wide variety of platforms or with Google for contributions to your keywords, or create a "Google Alert" and be notified about them.

129. Guest posts

⏱$

Guest posts, mostly via blogs, are a common way of creating varied content that is beneficial for everyone involved. If you promote these guest posts together and distribute them on your respective channels, then 1 + 1 often equals 4. If you make the decision to allow guest posts on your channels, above all to your blog and podcast, then you should also set rules which the guest author has to follow.

If you don't do that, your blog, your podcast, or your social media page could develop into an unstructured vendor's tray and that will damage your positioning.

The rules concern the type of content, minimum or maximum length, structure and spelling, keyword optimization, use of links (possible / not possible, follow / non follow), use of images or videos, and everything else that seems important to you.

If you can find writers who fit into your framework and follow your rules, this type of content creation can be very efficient.

130. Own guest contributions

⏱⏱$

Guest posts or articles from you on foreign channels is a strategy that can bring you many advantages as folllows:

- You get additional reach.
- You reach new target groups or people whom you would not reach through your own channels.
- You benefit from the, hopefully good, image of the foreign channel.

- You do not have to completely reinvent the post but can, as with blog posts, for example, adapt an existing post by rewriting, shortening, or extending it and thus save work and time.
- You will receive links, which you place in your guest post, to your page or your blog from which you will also benefit through new visitors to your website and a better Google ranking.

From this point of view, the strategy of placing your contributions in third-party channels is a very recommendable one in many cases. As for the content of these guest posts, you can use many of the strategies and ideas in this book.

Not only you, but also your host, will benefit from this approach. They will have new, different content that they don't have to write themselves and, like you, reaches new target groups if you distribute your guest post in your channels. A well-written, keyword-optimized guest post also helps with the Google ranking of their site or blog.

131. Swap accounts

🕐🕐$

As mentioned in an earlier chapter, it can be exciting and productive to swap accounts with another person for a specific, short period of time like a day or a week. This strategy brings variety and fresh momentum to your content and thus to the channel concerned. In concrete terms, this means you are using the social media profile of another person or company and the other is using yours.

This is a common practice on Instagram.However, it is also conceivable or feasible on other channels. The prerequisite for this, of course, are clear rules for both sides for exchanging accounts, and absolute mutual trust.

If you do it, don't do it in silence. Announce the account exchange to your online network, really celebrate it, and turn it into an event for yourself. Only then will you get the full benefit from this promotion.

132. Comments on third-party content

🕐$

Adding a comment to someone else's content in which you claim the opposite is already mentioned as a strategy in the "Impulse" section. But you can also use a very similar strategy by adding comments to other people's contributions that underline, praise, and/or add to what has been written or said.

The advantages that you have from this approach are manyfold:

- You create content quickly and easily.
- You build your expert status when you post technically good comments.

- You will get traffic to your site if you leave a link in the comment.
- You will become sympathetic to the author of the contribution (if you do not overdo it) and they will return the favor, if necessary, by leaving a comment on you. This can also result in further cooperation in online marketing.

This strategy can be implemented on all channels where there is a comment option. It is particularly recommended for blogs and social media, especially on high-reach channels.

If you basically like this idea, you should develop a well thought-out and planned strategy from it. Leaving a comment now and then is not enough. Include this as part of your editorial plan.

- Select the blogs, social media pages, groups (on Facebook, Pinterest, or LinkedIn) that fit you thematically or complement your business. That should be a larger number so that you don‘t comment too often on the same channels.
- Create a fixed rule of how often, where, and in what rhythm you want to comment.

Q.

Media

Media, like books and films, can be a great resource for new online content. You can use these in a number of ways. These can be books or films that are closely related to your business. Alternatively, they can be those that have nothing to do with your business, but with you as a person. This gives an insight into your preferences, an approach entirely in line with personal branding.

One point that can be a very powerful lever for many of the following ideas is the fact that the rights owner of the medium in question is, in many cases, very interested in their content being shared or distributed by you. Therefore, they might support you and thus help you to get more coverage.

133. Reviews including specialist books

⏱⏱**$**

If you read books or listen to audiobooks that are directly or broadly related to your business, then you can write about them. Such a book even provides material for a lengthy blog post or more than one post.

You can also involve the author here, so that both sides can benefit from it and increase both your reaches.

134. The best ideas from a book

⏱⏱**$**

In addition to reviewing a book, you could go a step further and summarize your key takeaways from the book and explain how to apply and implement them in your business.

135. Top lists of books

⏱**$**

You can also publish your own top lists in various subject areas, for example:

- as a manager or entrepreneur, the 10 top management books
- as a coach, the 10 top books on coaching, or ...personal growth
- as a fitness trainer, the 10 top books on muscle building, or ...nutrition, or also ... personal growth.

136. Movies, videos and podcasts

⏱**$**

You can basically do the same thing with movies as you can with books. It doesn‘t always have to be big films or series. YouTube videos or even podcasts are also suitable for this purpose.

Why not vote for and publish your personal top 10 YouTube videos on the subject of „personal growth?“

137. Online courses

🕐🕐$

Since there are more and more online courses available on different topics, these should also be mentioned here. If you have consumed an online course, you could report on it, review it and, if necessary, post your top learnings from it.

If the review is positive, the provider of the course is usually very interested in you and will provide you with active support.

R.

Interaction

In this chapter you will find a long list of ideas to encourage your contacts to interact with you more intensely and more often. Likes, for example, are good for your reach on social media, but comments and someone also sharing your post are much better. One of the most important goals in the context of the online placement of your content is therefore to produce articles and posts that are commented on and shared, or based on which your contacts become active in some form.

138. Polls

🕐🕐$

The opinion of others is often very interesting to people. Make surveys on your topics. If you keep this short (one to three questions), more people will answer. The effort to create surveys, is financially neither time consuming nor large. Tools like www.surveymonkey.com support you in this. In the simplest form, some social media channels also offer their own tools for creating surveys, which have the advantage that you can deliver the evaluation at the same time and make it visible to all users.

Make two out of one

You can implement a survey and its results as two separate activities. This is particularly recommended for larger surveys. First, post the survey asking for participation. Then, do the evaluation and post the results, divided into smaller pieces if necessary.

Example Black Friday study

For example, I did a large-scale Black Friday study where I asked my online contacts to join in, which worked out well. I processed the results in the form of a blog post and a series of social media posts. In addition, I made a press release with the results and thus received a number of articles in both online and offline media. As you can see, surveys are very productive when it comes to new content for your marketing.

Automated surveys

Another tried and tested variant are automated surveys. –For example, the way I do it is to automatically send a survey link to every new newsletter subscriber. It happens without human intervention. Good email marketing software can implement such automations easily and reliably. In this way, you can collect new answers for your survey every day, evaluate them at certain intervals, and share the results with your digital contacts.

139. Votes

🕐🕐$

You could say votes are a special variant of surveys. Your contacts will be asked for their opinion on specific alternatives. That could be three suggestions for book covers, three color suggestions for the new wall in your office, or which of four red wines you should serve at an upcoming event. In the perception of your contacts, however, votes are much more positive. Where surveys are often seen as an annoying additional task, votes are apparently a welcome interruption of everyday, boring routines. There are usually many comments and some provide additional ideas and variants.

140. „Fill in the blank“ posts

⏱$

A „fill in the blank“ post is a special type of question design. Such posts are mostly statements in half-sentence form with the request to complete the half-sentence. A few examples are:

- Donald Trump is ...
- For me, freedom means ...
- Even for a lot of money, I would never ...
- If I win $1M I will immediately ...
- For me, customer orientation means, above all, ...

This will motivate your contacts to be creative and you will quickly receive a series of varied and often very humorous comments.

In a second round you could even turn it into a small competition and ask everyone to like the answers that were given. The answer with the most likes wins a prize.

141. Questions to contacts

⏱$

In general, questions are a very good tool to activate your digital network. The different ways to ask questions are almost infinite. In particular, questions to which the respondents do not immediately know the answer, or questions to which there are many answers and which stimulate creativity, are exciting.

A number of examples can be found below:

- Preferences
- What is your favorite ... book, movie, actor, food, restaurant/pub, resort, apps ... and why?
- The future
- What will be an integral part of your everyday life in ten years? Where will you be in ten years?
- The past

What preoccupied you a year ago today? What did you wish for ten years ago that you have achieved today? If you could travel back in time ten years, which decision would you make differently or what would you change?

- **Things**
  Which five things can you least do without? What ten things would you definitely take with you to a desert island?

- **Problems** (for which you may have the solution)
  What is currently the biggest hurdle for you? What's the biggest problem in your industry?

- **Oneself**
  What are the three words that best describe you? What's on your bucket list?

- **Social media**
  Which social medium do you use the most and why? Which social medium could you safely do without and why?

- **Sports and exercise**
  How many kilometers do you walk in a week? How often do you exercise in a week? Do you take the stairs or the elevator?

- **"Famous firsts" or first times**
  What was your first car? What was your first cell phone? Where did your first flight go to? Who was the first customer you won over?

- **Innovations**
  What was the most important innovation for you in the last year (in the last five years, ten years etc.)

- **Technology**
  What three apps do you use the most? Which three apps did you recently delete?

- **Routines**
  What's the first thing you do in the morning? Which routines help you in your daily routine?

- **Productivity**
  What is your top tip for increasing productivity? What do you definitely avoid if you really want to achieve a lot?

- **Gratitude**
  What are you grateful for right now?

- **Business**
  Which insight/ three insights has/have had the most positive influence on you in business? How would you best invest $1,000 in your business? What project would you start if you knew it would work?

The series could be continued indefinitely. However, these questions should not only stimulate interaction and activate your contacts but can also provide you with concrete ideas and answers to topics and questions that you are dealing with.

In order to bring regularity and structure back into this idea, you could make it a question of the day or a question of the week (as is sometimes used in print media in connection with street surveys).

142. Requests

🕐$

Something formally similar to questions are requests that are sometimes asked as questions, but the intention behind them is different. The point is that you need support and help with something, or that you are looking for advice on something. The focus is not on activating your online contacts, although this is a nice side effect, but on real problem solving.

Things you can ask your community include:

- Ratings and reference statements on Google, Proven Expert, Facebook, Amazon, or another industry-specific rating platform.
- Contacts with certain companies or in certain industries. True to the BNI (Business International Network) motto, „I am looking for a contact with the marketing manager of company XY," or, „Who has contact with a fitness studio owner?"
- Recommendations from suppliers or service providers, for example "Who can recommend a good car painter?"

143. Networking contacts

🕐$

If you see an advantage in the fact that your own online contacts get to know and network better, then you can encourage this by, for example, introduce a different one of your contacts every day and ask the community to network with him or her and make friend requests. Ideally, of course, this is discussed in advance with the contact concerned.

144. Networking platforms

🕐$

You are connected to many of your contacts on multiple platforms, e.g. on Facebook, Instagram, and LinkedIn. This has the advantage that the likelihood that your contacts will see what you post also increases significantly. At the same time, there are a number of contacts with whom you are probably only connected on one platform, although they are also present on other channels.

In order to expand cross-platform networking, you can repeatedly make posts across your channels indicating that you are also present on Facebook, Instagram, etc. and would be happy to get in touch there too. Of course, you can also do this by individually going through contact by contact and searching on other platforms, but supporting this with posts can accelerate networking.

145. Competitions

🕐🕐🕐**$$**

Competitions, already mentioned at one point or another in the book, are a broad field of activity. You can create contests, post them, and potentially trigger a lot of interaction with your network. In fact, if the concept is good or funny, contests have a lot of potential to be shared. The really interesting thing about competitions, however, is that they result in a lot of pictures, videos, and articles, most of which are also posted by the competition participants themselves.

The competitions can be those that take place exclusively online, in which each participant documents and posts their participation in photographs or by video, or those that are implemented offline and also documented online.

146. Sweepstakes

🕐🕐🕐**$$**

The transition from competitions to sweepstakes is fluid. In a competition, however, there does not necessarily have to be something to win; in sweepstakes, prizes attract and encourage participation.

All kinds of competitions can be found online, serious as well as fake and, of course, fraudulent. But all three versions can succeed in getting a lot of likes, comments, and shares, even if it seems very obvious that it is a fake competition.

Online marketing expert Felix Beilharz has made it his business to expose such fake sweepstakes again and again and, by the way, achieves considerable reach and interactions with these posts.

This shows that sweepstakes, serious ones, can be an excellent tool as content for your channels in order to activate your digital contacts.

147. Chain letters

🕐🕐🕐**$$**

Chain letters existed long before the Internet. At that time, real letters or postcards were sent to several people who then each had the task of sending letters to a certain number of people under threat of seven years of bad luck or similar if they were not sent. These types of chain letters also exist in the online world and they are still just as annoying to many people.

And yet the thought has great potential for your online activities, as the chain letter mechanism is designed in a way that the number of participants increases exponentially. You name three people who should take part, each of them three more, etc. In the best-case scenario, this can create a viral wave that sweeps through the Internet.

You will surely remember the "ice bucket challenge," an example of a very successful campaign with a huge range. Since this challenge served a good cause even top politicians and celebrities of all kinds took part. Even if a chain letter of this kind rarely reaches this dimension, it is always worth trying if you have a funky and funny idea.

This should not advertise your product or your company too boldly, but there should always be a subtle yet real connection to you. There is a risk that you will succeed in a chain letter campaign, but nobody knows that it was yours, and that would be a shame.

148. Riddles and brain teasers

🕐🕐**$**

People are curious. Take advantage of this curiosity by giving them tasks that are not that easy or even very difficult to solve. Finding tricky questions and puzzles is not difficult, the challenge again is how to relate it to your business.

Such puzzles can be:

- Questions about your products or your industry,
  "How many muscles does the human body have?" (masseur)
- Estimation questions
  „How many of our delicious chocolate candies fit in this bathtub (show photo)?" - (confectionery manufacturer or retailer). You could also combine that with a competition, „Win a bathtub full of chocolate candies."
- Questions about fun facts
  „How many times a day do you swallow?" (brewery) „... and that works better if you do it with our beer."
- Crossword puzzle
  A crossword puzzle with terms from your topic would be an exciting idea for new content.
- Logic puzzles
  "What are the next two numbers 1, 3, 5, 7, 11 ...?"
- Arithmetic problems
  Even with arithmetic tasks that are a little trickier (but not too difficult), content can be created that encourages people to think and participate. It is not uncommon for such posts to produce ten or more answers, the vast majority of which contain the wrong result.

- Spelling puzzles
  If your business has anything to do with copywriting, such as proofreading or typing, you could create a series of difficult spelling questions. Your contacts can then give their opinion on the correct spelling before you reveal the solution.

- Picture puzzles
  A fairly simple type of picture puzzle can be created by taking a picture of an object or person related to your business and covering most of it. Then ask your online community what they think they see in the picture. You could also create this type of puzzle in stages by taking a series of pictures and revealing a bit more with each picture.

If you keep your eyes open and search social media platforms, daily newspapers and magazines, or simply Google for puzzles, you will come across many creative ideas that you can use for your business.

149. Creative tasks

🕐🕐**$**

Many more ideas can be found as a group than alone, and in a short time. You can use this fact not only to activate your contacts but also to source real ideas.

"What words for 'delicious' can you think of?" a food manufacturer or restaurateur could ask and thus activate the crowd and certainly receive a lot of comments on this post. At the same time, of course, the underlying message resonates, "Our food is delicious!"without having to specifically say or write that as an advertising message.

After many suitable terms have been collected, you can make a word cloud out of it and use it online in connection with your logo.

150. Geocaching - online / offline scavenger hunt

🕐🕐🕐**$$**

An online / offline scavenger hunt called geocaching causes more effort. "Geocaching is a kind of treasure hunt that began to spread at the end of the 20th century. The hiding spots are published on the Internet using geographic coordinates and can then be searched for using a GPS receiver.

A geocache is usually a watertight container that contains a logbook and, often, various small items for exchange. The visitor can enter themselves into a logbook to document their successful search. The geocache will then be hidden back in the place where it was previously found. What was found can then be noted on the Internet on the associated page and, if necessary, supplemented with photos.

In this way, other people, especially the hiding person or owner, can follow what is going on around the geocache.

It is essential in the entire search and exchange process that other people present do not recognize the project and so the geocache remains hidden from uninitiated people. In the spring of 2019, there should already be around three million participants in the variant game called „Cacher" (Wikipedia).

The advantage is that in many cases this game can be very well connected to your products or your business by using the geocache, for example fill it with your products or design it with your own design. There are so many options.

S.

Humor and entertainment

Humor is one of the best things both online and offline that gains reach, activates people to share, like, or comment, entertains, and creates positive feelings. Many of the other ideas in this book relate to humor.

Used with tact, it's always a good idea. But being funny and entertaining is not always easy and certainly not in a structured form or at the push of a button. Therefore, you will find some ideas and strategies below on how you can use humor in your content in a meaningful way.

In many cases you accidentally stumble upon humorous and funny sayings, pictures, videos, and texts of all kinds. It is best to create a few document files and make it a habit of collecting these things. You can then fall back on this collection when creating content.

151. Jokes

🕐🕐**$**

The classic when it comes to humor are jokes in written form or as videos. When jokes are good, people love to share them. To make it easier, it can be a good idea to turn the text into an image as text with a background.

152. Humorous sayings

🕐🕐**$**

Humorous sayings are also popular. It's best to have a collection of them. Whenever you see a saying that makes you smile or laugh, save it. The best thing to do is to come up with a standardized layout in which you only have to insert the respective saying and which you can use again and again. This allows you to prepare this post idea in advance and implement it quickly, and it also has a high recognition value.

153. Funny pictures

🕐🕐**$**

Of course, funny pictures are good reach charm. Especially when the humor is a little hidden, as in the picture with the market woman, it can work extremely well. The picture that I staged, took, and then posted in combination with a blog entitled "Do it like Amazon" worked extremely well as content. It gained more than two million viewers worldwide, more than 20,000 shares, and more than 100,000 likes. Interviews and reports about it appeared in many online and offline magazines and it was even part of an exhibition in the "Technical Museum Berlin."

The signs follow the Amazon cross-selling strategy. Customers who bought this also bought...

If you use images, please also refer to the observation of image rights at this point. In the event of violations, content creation could otherwise be significantly more expensive than planned.

154. Rhymes and poems

🕐🕐**$**

Anything that rhymes has the advantage that it is better noted and remembered. You too can pack your ideas, products, messages, or topics into short rhymes or longer poems.

On World Poetry Day I implemented an action with the poem, "The price Promotion." The, quite long, text was divided into individual stanzas and recorded by experts from various fields as a short video and then combined into a poem video (with subtitles).

Involving others, as in this example, again has the advantage of increasing your potential reach.

But you don't have to write or have someone write for you. If you make a connection to your business you can also use poems of all kinds to create content (taking into account any rights of the authors, of course). Why not use excerpts from classic poems that you may have had to learn in school and relate them to your business.

155. Cartoons

🕐🕐**$$**

Cartoons can be a very popular content. There are a number among which you will find something for your business (but pay attention to image rights!). The Simpsons, Peanuts, and Garfield are classics that, when tailored to your situation, can result in humorous content. Drawing cartoons yourself, or having them drawn, is also an option, although of course more complex.

156. Reprogrammed music

🕐🕐🕐$

Most songs are entertaining but not funny. One strategy for making pieces of music humorous is to rewrite the text. For example, many songs have been provided with texts appropriate to Corona and recorded during the Covid-19 crisis. Many of them are really successful and some are very funny.

A good example of this, which has had more than five million views on YouTube within eight weeks, can be found here: https://www.youtube.com/watch?v=8KPbJ0-DxTc. Especially in difficult times, a successful, humorous discussion of the problems is often rewarded with a long reach and a lot of interaction.

157. Fun facts

🕐🕐$

The fun facts mentioned in a previous chapter are also a type of humor that can work well to create popular online content.

Here are a few examples of how you can use completely nonsensical and weird facts for your content marketing:

- "Banging your head against the wall for an hour burns 150 calories," Could use a gym to better suggest alternatives to burning calories. Incidentally, this could also be used to make a very nice series with completely nonsensical activities, each of which indicates how many calories are burned with it.
- "In Switzerland it is illegal to keep only one guinea pig." A nice fun fact for a pet shop.
- "7% of Americans believe that chocolate milk comes from brown cows." That would be worth a nice post from a farm, dairy, or grocery company.

158. Top 10 lists

🕐🕐$

We already mentioned "Top 10 lists" in another context. But, if you want it to be funny and entertaining, you can use top 10 lists by collecting and listing quirky and funny top candidates:

- "The 10 Most strong smelling foods" could be posted by a room spray maker.
- "The 10 slowest officials" as content for a productivity coach.
- "The 10 ugliest dogs" would make a nice series for a dog groomer or a pet shop.
- "The 10 most serious spelling mistakes in print media" would be something that a tutoring institute could use very well.

- “The 10 fastest orgasms (e.g. based on peoples, cultures, and nationalities)” would be a potentially widely read post for a manufacturer of sex toys.

Which weird “Top-10-lists” can you create for your industry or your product?

159. Children

⏱⏱$

When using children in your online content you must, of course, be particularly careful. But that doesn‘t mean it can‘t work. Done well, you can produce great, entertaining, and often very funny content with children.

- Children could e.g. define terms from your industry in front of the camera.
- You can let the children draw these terms.
- Another idea might be to give the same drawing task to several children and turn the results into a nice series of picture posts.
- Children in funny disguises on photograph or film bring you potentially many ’likes,’ but also guarantees you the eternal hatred of children once they are grown up and see the painful and embarrassing photos. As long as they are not your own children it can, in principle, leave you indifferent. Still, it can also be a strategy, e.g. for a temporary employment agency that arranges jobs in the technical and manual sectors and puts children in the appropriate work clothes for the photos.
- Let children build your Lego product or make variants of it. You can then also combine that with a competition.

If you work with children and you organize competitions, for example, then, of course, you also have the parents on your side. Many an ambitious parent naturally wants their child to win the competition and supports this on their channels as best they can.

160. Animals

⏱⏱$

Animal photos as a reach broker were already mentioned in chapter 12. Because animals can also be used very well in the area of humor (e.g. animals in disguise), I am pointing it out again at this point.

161. Games

⏱⏱⏱$$

Games do not necessarily have to be funny, but they must be entertaining. Gamification—the application of elements and procedures that are typical for games in situations and areas that have nothing to do with games per se—has become very popular in recent years. For example, games have found their way into what used to be very conservative or traditional management training courses.

If you want to use games as content for your online channels, however, in many cases solid effort is involved. At the same time, a successful game can be used in the form of an app e.g. activate a lot of people. One way can also be to transfer simple games that are very well known and widespread offline into the online world, or create highly simplified forms of well-known games that can be displayed well online.

162. Unboxing videos or photos

🕐🕐$

Unboxing videos or photos are also not necessarily funny, but still entertaining and welcome. Film or photograph the receipt and / or unpacking of a mail item. Authors love doing this when they have their latest books delivered to them.

Your bonus tip

the book. In the best-case scenario, our head or your notepad are full of great ideas for exciting content that fits your business perfectly. You may even have more of it than you can handle. That would then be a so-called luxury problem.

But it wouldn´t be me if I didn´t save one idea and one strategy for last. As mentioned at the beginning, we live in times that are very loud and dense in the media. And yes, you have to do a lot more and be more creative than you did a few years ago to get noticed. Yet, it has to be okay from time to time not to post anything and to deliberately take a break. An hour, a day, or a week, depending on how tight your editorial schedule is.

But you can, if you want, stage that. Announce this absence or time-out online, turn it into a bit of content and then tell a story true to the motto “What happened when I was not online.“

Or treat yourself to the luxury—which is increasingly becoming THE luxury par excellence—to be completely offline for once. Just because.

Good luck with your posting and may the reach be with you!

Yours

Roman Kmenta

About the author

Marketing and pricing expert Roman Kmenta has been an international entrepreneur, keynote speaker, and bestselling author for more than 30 years. The business economist and serial entrepreneur makes his many years of international marketing and sales experience in the B2B and B2C sectors available to over 100 top companies and many small businesses and sole proprietorships in Germany, Switzerland, and Austria.

Photo: Matern, Vienna

More than 25,000 people read his blog or listen to his podcast every week. Through his lectures he gives salespeople, executives, and entrepreneurs food for thought on the subject of „profitable growth" and gives his listeners and readers inspiration towards a value-oriented sales and marketing approach.

www.romankmenta.com

Find your USP and become unique!

Endless competitors, and all of them offer the same thing - at least from the point of view of many customers.

Positioning, differentiating yourself, and being unique, are all becoming increasingly important for many companies. Essential for survival. It is important to find unique selling points, ideally a USP, a unique value proposition.

In this book you will get:

- A tried and tested strategy on how to find your market positioning and USP.
- Ideas on how to unmistakably present your customer benefits.
- Tips on how to shine through uniqueness and clearly stand out from the mediocre.
- Strategies used by top brands to create differentiators.
- Over 500 specific USP examples to set you apart from your competition.

To be better than the competition is good. But the best strategy for higher sales, fees, and income is to be different. Best of all, unique.

Order here >>

Amazon.com - https://amzn.to/2FP4Ijg

Amazon.co.uk - https://amzn.to/33VqQ3h

Amazon.com.au - https://amzn.to/3mNZzso

Amazon.ca - https://amzn.to/2G2pknK

"In this book you will not only find the generally valid explanations about the USP, but also numerous practical examples that can be adapted immediately for your particular business case. The book is not only aimed at pure USP rookies, but also at those who have already started to think about it and are looking for further impulses. Although I haven't only been dealing with USP since yesterday, I have received valuable suggestions. Highly recommended. „

Leopold Pokorny, ECDL project manager

www.elege.online / www.mentor.at

As Amazon partner I earn commission on qualified sales.

THE
MARKET
POSITIONING
BOOK
500+ TRIED AND TESTED IDEAS INCLUDED
500+ creative ideas on how to easily find your Unique Selling Proposition and differentiate from the Competition
ROMAN KMENTA

Never speechless anymore in price talks

That's too expensive! Do you hear that again and again in price negotiations? You will find 118 answers to price objections in this book so that you are never speechless again in price discussions. You will always have the right answer ready for handling objections. The spectrum goes from cheeky to convincing, from sensible and calculated to humorous ... in any case, profitable!

With this book you will:

- Always find the right answer to objections in price negotiations.
- Get to know new negotiation techniques and methods of handling objections.
- Learn to use psychological tips and strategies effectively in price negotiations.
- Make your negotiations more successful.
- Get better results when negotiating prices.
- Have more fun negotiating prices.

Reader votes

„From pragmatic to emotional, cheeky and, above all, implementable for a wide variety of industries and situations.“

“Sales are often about reframing and eloquence. You can tell that the long list has arisen from a wealth of experience that is second to none. „

„Top! - I have already attended many expensive seminars and received far fewer sayings that can be used in practice.“

„Cheeky, innovative, brave, and confidently sell your value!“

„Seldom laughed so much and found so much again!“

PRICE OBJECTION
HANDLING
MADE
EASY
118 Proven Sales Tactics
that Never Leave You
Speechless in a
Price Negotiation
ROMAN KMENTA

Top strategies to enforce higher prices

Achieving higher prices is a key success factor for most companies. A very special challenge is to carry out price increases with existing customers in such a way that the customer remains a customer. It is important to know about and implement a number of decisive strategies in sales and marketing.

This book is dedicated to these strategies. Pricing and price increases are issues that affect the entire company. Accordingly, some of the recommended approaches are comprehensive, far-reaching, and in-depth. At the same time, you will also find tips in this book that can be implemented quickly and easily, which will make the next price increase easier and bring you a lot of money.

In this book you will learn:

- when the optimal time is for a price increase
- how not to make a price increase look like one
- how to avoid price comparability
- how to increase the value of your offer in the eyes of the customer
- how to avoid price negotiations
- which price psychological affects you should be aware of
- which arguments you can use to support a price increase
- how to raise prices without raising prices.

Higher prices, higher contribution margins, and more income. A book that pays off.

„Order here >>

Amazon.com - https://amzn.to/3r5ZUsM
Amazon.co.uk - https://amzn.to/3i6OFMC
Amazon.com.au - https://amzn.to/2T7T0H3
Amazon.ca - https://amzn.to/3AZvcGg

ROMAN KMENTA
CHARGE MORE EARN MORE
How to confidently increase prices without losing customers
A practical sales guide for managers, entrepreneurs and salespeople.
BUSINESS IN A NUTSHEL
Practical knowledge in a compact form.

Create written offers that win

Written offers are a greatly underestimated instrument in the sales process. A lot of companies produce many of them, but pay little attention to them. Offers are silent salespeople, who spend more time with or at the customer, than the sales force in some business areas and industries.

So how can you raise the potential that lurks in your offers and turn them into better sellers? How can you design your offers to convince your customers?

In this book you will learn

- why your customers basically don‘t care about your offer and what they are really interested in
- how to build up offers effectively in terms of sales psychology
- how your offers can be made much more attractive with the right design
- what the most promising ways of delivering your offers are
- which price psychological strategies you use to make your offers appear more favorable
- how you clearly differentiate yourself from your competitors through your offers
- what a „Shock and Awe Package“ is and how you can use it in a targeted manner.

Better offers bring more sales to a close. A book that pays off.

Order here >>

Amazon.com - https://amzn.to/3kd88xV

Amazon.co.uk - https://amzn.to/2TWWWLj

Amazon.com.au - https://amzn.to/2VDI5FW

Amazon.ca - https://amzn.to/3kjdyaR

As Amazon partner I earn commission on qualified sales.

ROMAN KMENTA
HOW TO
WRITE OFFERS
THAT SELL
44
psychological
strategies to create
a successful offer
A practical sales guide for
managers, entrepreneurs
and salespeople
BUSINESS IN A
NUTSHEL
Practical knowledge
in a compact form.

Printed in Great Britain
by Amazon

86988353R00095